life lessons, love lessons

LIFE LESSONS, LOVE LESSONS

*A Guru's Daughter Discovers
Knowledge Is Only Half the Journey*

KAMINI DESAI

Red Elixir, Rhinebeck, New York ❧ Inner Source, Salt Springs, Florida

Book design by Georgia Dent
Cover design by Deborah DeFranco: artpulse@comcast.net

Library of Congress Control Number: 2010939051
ISBN: 978-0-9830517-0-1

Red Elixir in association with Epigraph Publishing
22 E. Market Street
Suite 304
Rhinebeck, New York 12572
USA 845-876-4861

To my life teachers in the many roles you have played.

Thank you.

Life is an Enchanting Journey
of Unconditional Love

THE EXPERIENCE OF LOVE is what we seek in every expression of life. It is the inborn, evolutionary urge to merge that guides us to search for love in countless ways. We search everywhere; we explore every possible way to find it. We would give anything to get it; we are willing to lose everything to have it.

This insightful book by my daughter, Kamini Desai, is the lifelong culmination of years of study, practice, teaching, living and loving. She was born into a spiritual lineage and was exposed to the highest yogic teachings since her first breath. Growing up in an ashram, she was showered with the sacred ancient teachings passed down to me from my guru, and to him from his guru. Even though the teachings came from the highest, I was on my own spiritual journey and learning through living.

Kamini was on her own journey through her formative years. I attempted always to guide her with all the knowledge I had in the best possible way, but I was an amateur parent and replicated what I believed was proper parenthood from my Indian heritage. In retrospect, this prevented me from truly integrating what I was teaching. A clash of cultures created a conflict from which we both suffered. In retrospect, I would have managed my role differently as both a father and a guru.

Over time, Kamini learned from me and I from her. We are mirrors, showing each other what we each need to know — all that is beautiful and ugly, good and bad, sacred and profane.

We have matured in our capacity to delve into the inner depth of our relationship. Much of the credit for our personal growth goes to Kamini and her ability to hold the space for me to work through the challenges we have faced. This is the process of spiritual growth – accepting each other and ourselves with open hearts and unconditional love. Through our conscious interactions we have both evolved, growing closer, working together and respecting each other. I am so touched by her courage to reveal herself so honestly. Her conscious journey through loving relationships can serve as a guide to readers in their own process of self-discovery.

The secret of love is that the moment you demand love, it disappears and conflict appears. When you simply give, conflict disappears and love reappears. Love gives you back what you are willing to put into it.

At its highest, love is the most powerful force and an evolutionary journey. Love embraces life's ups and downs, both the spiritual and mundane, providing openings to manifest its miracles.

In the beginning, love may appear to be crawling through a caterpillar stage. Even though it appears to build its own cocoon, it is not a trap but a transformative process that gives wings to the earthbound love. When grounded in purity and unconditional giving, love goes beyond all dreams and reveals reality.

Ultimately, intimate relationships represent the relationship you have with yourself. They demand nothing less than the death of the ego. Intimacy is a mirroring relationship, where everything that was invisible is made visible.

> *Instead of asking for love, be loving.*
> *Instead of searching for peace, be peaceful*
> *Instead of wanting to be loved, be loving.*
> *Instead of waiting to be understood, be understanding.*
> *Instead of looking for attention, be attentive.*
> *Instead of seeking acceptance, be accepting.*

Love is complete within itself. Love is not an exchange; it is unconditional giving. It does not wait for a return. Anything you expect in exchange turns it into a commodity in the marketplace. When you give fully from your heart, you are fulfilled in the giving.

The words of my beloved teacher, Bapuji, concisely summarize this great awareness of oneself: "The key that unlocks your heart is hidden in the heart of the other. Only when unconditional love creates an opening in the heart of another, will you find the key that unlocks your own heart."

— *Yogi Amrit Desai*

INTRODUCTION

A s young women in the West, we live and breathe the romantic ideal of love. The unspoken given is that some day, just like Cinderella and her prince, we will be pulled out of the doldrums of our everyday existence and catapulted into a life of infinite and unending love where we will be loved and live in contentment, peace and happiness forever. We will bask in the sunshine of our beloved and through him we will feel whole. Reinforced through innumerable modern re-runs of fairytales–Harlequin romance novels, Love Boat episodes, and movies of Pretty Woman ilk, we fall victim to an ideal that makes our life appear as if it somehow does not measure up.

Fairytale love implies finding wholeness in, or through, another. It is based on an assumption that we can create an experience of completion through another that we do not possess ourselves. If we could stop looking at our lives through the promise of the fairytale, we might find we have gotten it backwards. We have always been in possession of our own completeness. It is only the assumption that "I don't have it and you need to give it to me," which has made us overlook the possibility for fulfillment that has always been present. In other words it is the *belief* in the fairytale itself, the idea that someone out there will "save me," that keeps us from saving ourselves–from realizing we ourselves are the key to finding the completion we are searching for.

WHAT IS THE KEY?

Romance is one of the most powerful ideals we hold as a society. It is all-pervading, filtering into every aspect of our lives from movies, to books, to pop culture and magazines. Once adopted, anything but that ideal appears lacking. This is why an enduring perception lingers in our society that people who are alone cannot possibly be happy–and those who are in a relationship must, by definition, be more so. It is why some women who are alone past a certain age feel they have "missed their window," as if there is only a limited time to find a mate, and therefore happiness. Perhaps it is why the successful career woman who doesn't want a relationship is looked upon with vague distrust. "How could she possibly be happy?" people ask.

The truth is, minus comparison to a romantic ideal, all of these could be perfectly satisfying states of being. Yet when we insist on a picture of romantic love as the pinnacle of achievement in the personal realm, everything else seems to pale in comparison. No matter how well our life may be working, or how fulfilling the other aspects of our life may be, the idea we *should* have something more makes what we have look like less. If we could let go of our romantic ideal of how it should be and let it be the way it is, we would automatically experience peace and contentment with the way things are right now—single, married, dating or divorced. None of it is an impediment to our happiness *until* we compare it to the ideal we have created in our own minds.

THE ROAD TO UNHAPPINESS
HAPPENS THROUGH COMPARISON

This phenomenon also extends to relationships we are already in. If we are currently in a relationship, but it is not measuring up to our idea of how it should be fulfilling us, it appears something is "wrong" with the relationship. We feel we have to do something to "fix" it. The truth is that, like all things, the way we interact with others will give rise to all kinds of experiences, some high and some low. This is just the natural order of things. But instead of allowing for the natural ups and downs that make up life, we compare those ups and downs to our picture of how it could or should be. It is through our comparison to that picture that we become unhappy and dissatisfied with what we have. In other words, most of the time nothing is wrong with our lives; everything is just fine. Just as waves have crests and valleys, so do our lives and our relationships. It is only by virtue of comparison to our ideal that what we have appears as a problem.

When circumstances, or our loved ones, don't quite fit our picture we try to fix them, train them, and eventually if they really don't cooperate, we get rid of them. In some cases that is a valid and necessary choice. However, for many of us there is another equally valuable option. We can learn to let go of our picture of how things should be. We can develop the skill of just being with things as they are. We can stop comparing and start appreciating.

We Try to Plan to Be Happy

As women, we may pick up other pictures as well. Perhaps it is the image of the ideal mother or wife, the picture of the career woman–smart and successful–creating her own independence and wealth. We decide that when we achieve this picture, when we've accomplished everything this picture stands for, we will have arrived–and then we will be happy. So we go about trying to fit ourselves, and our lives, into that picture. Once we manage to make it happen we tell ourselves we will be able to relax and enjoy.

Dutifully we study, and we excel. We work, we mother, and we care for our partners. We put in our dues and slowly become skilled in our chosen direction. But somehow the closer we come to that idealized picture, the further it seems to recede on the horizon. One piece falls into place and another falls out. We find ourselves in a constant state of juggling to get things to "fit" our picture. We get frustrated with ourselves and with others. We are willing to spend days, months and years of tying ourselves up in knots for that one moment when everything will fall into place. As a result, our life begins to feel like long periods of suffering, misery and stress, occasionally broken by those rare moments when everything is in its place. Only then do we feel we can relax.

Michael Singer, a modern sage, once pointed out that in case we have not caught on, life has no allegiance to our plans. It simply comes and goes. When conditions come together in certain ways, certain people, paired with certain circumstances, combined with timing–things happen. It is like a weather system that results from the coalescence of air pressure, temperature, wind direction and speed. Depending on how the factors come together, we get sun, rain, storms and clouds. They are not good or bad; they are simply the natural outcome of forces coming together in a certain way. Life is the same way. It simply unfolds according to the forces acting on it at any given moment. To expect the forces of nature to conform to our individual plan is foolhardy. And to rest our happiness on something that is by its nature mercurial, is even more so. It's no wonder so many of us are anxious and worried! If we are completely dependent on the forces of nature to come together in such a way to fit our ideal of happiness, we should be worried. We *should* be anxious. We are in a precarious position. Our fulfillment seems to rest in the hands of fate–but only if we are depending on conditions to make us happy.

If we are reliant on external situations to make us happy, we can only be happy when they are present. If we have decided we will be happy when we lose twenty pounds, finally find that relationship, or get our partner to change, we are also implicitly saying we *cannot* be happy until these things happen. Suddenly, we are dependent on those things as the source of our happiness, and we have to go out and get them. We become a slave to circumstances.

WE ARE THE AGENTS OF OUR OWN DISCONTENT

The funny thing is, we are the ones who manufacture these requirements. Who decided if the scale says 125, we can be happy? And if it says 165 we can't? We decide. Those are simply numbers. What we make of them is our own choice. We set the bar. If our partner learns to be financially responsible or more considerate, we can be happy. But if they don't change, we can't be happy.

So then, why do we do this? To motivate change. To get to the picture we think will make us happy, we have to be unhappy about the way things are now. We think we have to hate our bodies to get them more fit and healthy. We don't trust that we can transform our bodies if we begin by loving them as they are. Once we get into the habit of *creating through negating*, we tend to do it with everything. We try to create relationships by being unhappy with not having one. We try to improve relationships by complaining about the way they are, or wishing they were different. This only perpetuates dissatisfaction in the name of the fulfillment we seek.

Recognizing we are actually the greatest agents of our own discontent is not something to be depressed about. It is, in fact, *empowering*. If we have gotten into the habit of rating our satisfaction by the presence or absence of externals, we can also choose to withdraw from the habit. We can stop deciding we'll only be happy when our pictures are met. We can decide to be at peace with how things are now *and* if our goals happen to be realized.

That doesn't mean we can't make changes. The question is, can we make them from a place of willingness to accept that, for now, things are the way they are? Can we lose weight by first accepting and loving ourselves as we are now, *and* at the end when we reach our goal? Can we find fulfillment in our relationships as they are, *and* still make changes in the direction we want to go? This is a formula for creating a life that builds upon wholeness and satisfaction as its basis.

The Secret Weakness

I grew up as the daughter of a Guru. I learned all the wisdom the ancients had to offer from the time I could walk. I became a teacher of life skills; communication, conflict resolution, team-building, stress management, wellness and work-life balance. I was good, and over time, I got better. Anyone looking at me would have thought I was "together." I was a woman confidently charting the course of her own life. But I had a secret–I was still yearning for the "fairytale" picture, and the man who would fit perfectly into my carefully constructed life story. So no matter how great my successes, I always felt a tiny bit empty. I felt my story was not complete.

This "secret" became the source of my weakness. It was based upon an assumption that by comparison to this secret desire, my life was not good enough. In that comparison alone, my life felt incomplete—when in fact it was not so. I was also implicitly stating that someone else had the power to give me something I couldn't give myself. That was how I ended up in relationships where I lost the essence of who I was so totally, I became a shell of the woman I was. I lost my power, my spark, everything that made me beautiful and strong. I gave it all up in the hopes of that secret conviction.

Though I rationally knew better, I unconsciously believed if I could find that perfect relationship, my life would be complete. I gave up everything, including myself, for that picture. And I did it not once, but twice. I was convinced if I could just change my life to fit my storybook picture, and get my partners to play the imaginary roles I had created for them, it would all be perfect.

MEASURING UP

My dream formula for happiness was simple. Be the right woman, and find the right man. He would give me unconditional love, unconditional acceptance, unconditional presence. But first, to be the "right" woman, I had to fit the ideal I had manufactured in my head. I had to deny who I was—because I certainly wasn't perfect. To motivate myself to move towards this perfect image, I withheld love from myself until I could match it. Since that could never realistically happen for any length of time, I denied myself the things I wanted most; acceptance, love, contentment, and peace. I cut myself off from my own source—in the name of finding it from someone else.

This self-imposed separation from love only fueled my need to experience it through someone else. But not only had I effectively cut myself off from receiving my own love, I also cut myself off from anyone who might actually love me. After all, if

I didn't fit my own picture of how I should be, how could I be lovable to anyone else?

This set me up in a strange catch-22. When I finally received the love I so desperately wanted, I was unable to fully receive it because I was convinced I did not really deserve it. No matter how many compliments I received, how much I was told I was loved, some small corner in me believed I was still not good enough. I believed I didn't deserve love because I couldn't measure up to my own standards of lovability. In my search for becoming the image of the perfect person who was deserving of a perfect life, I undercut everything that could have given me just that.

THE POSSIBILITY OF TRUE LOVE

Lest this start sounding cynical, let me say I am a romantic and an optimist at heart. I believe love is a powerful presence that has the potential to transform our lives. But the twists and turns of my life have led me to realize one thing.

Most of us think that people and experiences unfolding in certain specific ways are responsible for our experience of love. This creates dependency. But this dependency is an illusion. It is not that I don't believe in love, I no longer believe dependency on another is the only way to experience it. In fact, love is something, that when understood, can be experienced anywhere, at any time. Like the sun that is always shining, love is always accessible. But we as human beings tend to close our windows when our conditions aren't met and shut it out. It doesn't mean it is not there, but simply that we have chosen not to be open to its presence. If we can increase our capacity to remain open under circumstances that would normally shut us down to love, we can experience more of it in our lives.

The possibility of love is not person-dependent. Single, married, dating, divorced, thick, thin, successful or failure; everyone possesses equal access to love. Love is an experience of being so totally fulfilled by a moment that all conflicts fade, all resistance dissolves. We merge into the moment so totally that nothing else matters. We enter a timeless state where the past falls away and dreaming about the future is unnecessary. When in love, the rest of our life doesn't change, but it feels as if it has. We don't just fall in love with a person; we fall in love with life. We are more open to every person we meet, every encounter we have. We are better able to flow with daily obstacles. This is because the experience of love happens *within us*. Sometimes another person is an agent of opening to life in that way. Sometimes it is an event, a great song or a stunning sunset.

The point is, we are the ones who decide if we experience love or not. And those decisions change from moment to moment. We can experience a loving, open-hearted feeling with someone one day and lose all memory of that love the next day when they've forgotten our birthday. The other person has not essentially changed. What has shifted is our *choice* to be open to the other person as they are. When we choose not to be open to the other as they are, we lose our love connection. This gives us a clue as to how and why we are always the masters of love in our lives.

The more we choose to remain open to our loved ones, partners, colleagues, and life events, the more love we will experience. Instead of relying on the other to create the circumstances that allow us to feel love, we decide to love outside of circumstance.

It is as simple as that. Another word for this is unconditional love, but I hesitate to use it because it has so many preconceived connotations. It does not mean we suppress our own needs and wants. It means we begin by allowing ourselves to be as we are with the needs we have, while allowing the other person to be who they are.

Like many of us, I didn't realize I always had the love I was seeking. I was ignoring the very simple truth that I was capable of being fulfilled by what I already had and who I already was. I spent many years trying to achieve the "perfect me" with the "perfect man" when all I had to do was open my heart fully to myself and to my life, exactly as it was.

This book interweaves the stories of three relationships. The first two are accounts of my journeys through the two major romantic relationships of my life that finally led me back to my roots and eventually to the seed of the truest relationship—with myself. It is a fairytale in reverse. A story of a girl, who goes out to find her prince only to find that no matter how handsome, how perfect, and how much he loves her, he can never give her what she is ultimately looking for. Only after years of wishing and waiting did I recognize that I would never find what I wanted. Not because it wasn't there, but because it wasn't to be found where I was looking for it. Only then, did I come back to where the whole mis-"take" began. I "took" the other to be my source.

When I took myself back, I found love. I found wholeness. I found the fulfillment I was always searching for. My prince charming resides within me. I have the power to give myself security and love under all circumstances. The oneness, the merging I was seeking was within, and a part of me that was always there and never missing. It was me all along. I just never noticed it because I was so busy giving myself up so I could find something out there. This is the story of how I figured it out.

Even now as I write this, there is a certain feeling of shame. A rational knowledge that this *shouldn't* have been the case. I *should* have known or recognized my own gifts without needing anyone to validate them. I *shouldn't* have needed to spend years on the circuitous route of trying to find someone who would fulfill the simple task of urging me to be myself. I *should* have just done that from the very beginning. But I didn't. I did it this way. And as much as others, and even myself, might argue it would have been smarter to do it differently, it is not the way I did it. I did it the way I did it, and I learned what I needed to as a result.

CHAPTER ONE

HAVING A GURU as a father, I was brought up as spiritual royalty. A princess of sorts, in a spiritual dynasty. One might think having access to spiritual truths from a young age would bring instant transcendence, leading to a perfectly painless life filled with peace and joy. Nothing could be further from the truth. I had to learn my lessons just like everyone else. Everyone does.

My father met his spiritual teacher, Bapuji, when he was 16 years old. From that time, he devoted himself to the teachings of that tradition. Over the years, he became one of Bapuji's closest students and was eventually one of only four, chosen from thousands of followers, to carry his teachings of the ancient tradition of yoga to the world. These ancient traditions had been transferred to Bapuji from his own teacher through secret practices and teachings; the depth of which were personally revealed through time, and with experience.

Because these teachings were passed from the teacher to a chosen few disciples, it was known as a lineage. The basis of that lineage was simple. Regardless of our history, religion, or ethnicity, there are a few eternal truths that can help us live a life of greater ease, peace and happiness. We cause ourselves undue suffering when we are out of alignment with these basic life principles. These were the truths this tradition of yoga sought to share with the world, seeing the whole world as one family.

My father had an arranged marriage to my mother at the age of 22. At 5' 11" he was tall for an Indian man, with strong features; a square jaw, high cheekbones and dark arresting eyes that flashed against his golden skin. His lean, fit physique was courtesy of the yoga he had learned from his teacher and his natural talent for sports of all kinds. For a time he'd even joined the Indian Air Force for the arduous physical training.

My mother was a diminutive 4 feet 11 inches. Her baby-soft skin, softly rounded cheeks, gently sloped nose and waving long black hair made the perfect foil of feminine beauty to my father's striking masculine looks.

Being an art student, my father moved with my mother to a larger city near their hometown in India. There he taught at a Catholic school, in addition to private tutoring and any other jobs he could get. He had no car and would ride his bicycle to get around, my mom sitting on the back, elegantly wrapped in her sari.

My father's dream was to come to America. It was all he had ever wanted and spoke about. Finally, after years of applying, he received a highly coveted scholarship and a student visa to go to the United States. Unable to borrow the money from his uncle, who told him he did not have a "travel line" upon reading his palm, my father promptly said he'd make his own line. He sold his watch, his bicycle and everything he had of worth to buy his plane ticket to America. He'd have about enough money in his pocket to last one week and the address of the friend of a friend where he might stay for a few days.

Going to his teacher Bapuji, he asked for his blessing. Bapuji gave him more. He told him it was his destiny to bring the teachings he had received to the West, and some day he would be considered one of the great pioneers of the authentic teachings of yoga in the West. Unsure he could make this happen my father nonetheless accepted his teacher at his word. Eventually the prophetic message faded from memory.

Lacking funds to pay for my mother's ticket to the U.S. and unable to provide for the both of them, my father went to America on his own. He landed in Philadelphia. Only able to speak rudimentary English, he had gotten off at the wrong bus stop in the middle of winter and had walked the last 20 blocks to his address in sandals and a loose cotton shirt. He had never seen snow and could never have imagined the cold. No one from his town had ever been to the U.S. No one could tell him how to prepare or what to expect. Finally making it to the address of the one contact he had, he was shown to a simple room and promptly asked for rent. This would not be a free ride.

Going to school by day and finding a job as a cafeteria busboy by night, he lived as sparingly as he could, squeezing out only the smallest amount of toothpaste on his brush and saving slivers of soap. Any additional money he had he sent to his wife, who was now living with his mother.

Finally, my mother was able to come to the U.S. with my father's brother, Shanti. The three of them began working; my mother taking care of the house and a young son, my father as a textile designer, and my uncle, Shanti as a chemist. Shanti married and eventually the two couples lived together.

On the side, my father, remembering the teachings he'd received, began conducting yoga classes. Shanti taught as well. With hard work the two of them built up a yoga society which trained 51 yoga teachers to help them lead 150 yoga classes a week in every YMCA, YWCA and community center in the Philadelphia area. In that time, around 1970, yoga was essentially unheard of. One hundred and fifty full classes a week was phenomenal. In this time another son was born, and a few years after, I was born.

In 1972, my father had a spiritual awakening that changed his understanding and perspective on yoga forever. His teacher, confirming his experience, told him to deepen his studies and his practice. When I was five years old, he decided to leave everything he had built and buy a place to retreat to in Pennsylvania Dutch Country, outside Philadelphia. But instead of having time to go into his own spiritual reflection, his students followed, and so began a yoga retreat center. At first it was four people, then 10, then 20 and continued to grow from there.

In the beginning when we moved to the yoga center, we all lived in a converted garage underneath the group common room. My father and mother had their own room. My brothers had bunk beds and I had a mattress on the floor; though often I would sleep with my mother instead. My brothers and I coexisted quite effortlessly. My clothes were kept under the sink in the bathroom for lack of space.

As the center grew, my mother was taking care of more and more responsibilities; rising at the crack of dawn to begin baking bread and preparing meals for the residents. My father was still doing some teaching in the surrounding area and my mother would roast nuts, make granola, and bag the extra homemade bread for sale at my father's classes. When I was old enough my mother left me to my own devices on the property. I would occupy myself with any of the student residents who would play with me—on the swings, in the garden, with pretend tea parties. Each member of the community contributed to my education in a different way and I felt very free and safe among them.

At night we would all gather for an evening of chanting songs and yoga teaching. As a child this was ideal. Other kids and I would run around in the back of the room during the chanting, then would return to sit with our parents during the lecture portion. My father would guide the evenings, my mother off to his left on an area rug. I would sit there with my mother listening to everything my father said until my eyes would droop and my head would begin to nod. She would put my head in her lap and I would fall asleep to the sound of my father's voice. One of the students would carry me downstairs and put me in bed every night after the evening session.

We had no T.V. until I was 11 years old. My entertainment was books, drawing, my imaginary world and playing in the woods. A resident student would tell me stories every night before the evening session. I would lie on a stack of unrolled bedrolls in the back of the common room and pretend I was the "princess and the pea" while he would recount the next episode in the continuing saga of the "fairy princess and her pearl necklace." Every night I listened to the life principles my father was teaching. Once he asked me if I could understand what he was saying. I replied that of course I could. He was surprised.

Eventually, the center grew too large and expanded to another location in Pennsylvania. This center not only offered yoga programs, but holistic health education programs including conscious eating, detoxification programs, counseling, massage trainings, aerobic exercise and more. A health center featured massage, sauna, whirlpool and facials, the precursor to our modern-day spas. It was on the cutting-edge of what would become part of mainstream health maintenance thirty years later.

In the summer, parents would come and take programs while kids could participate in the children's program, which included arts and crafts, hiking, hay rides, games and swimming. This was how I grew up. Even then I was treated differently. I could join the kids program, but I could come and go as I pleased. I was allowed to join the other "grown-up" programs as long as I participated fully and fulfilled all the class requirements. Having developed an early interest, I took my first massage training when I was fourteen years old. I was a kid, but not quite. I was the Guru's daughter.

Through the years as the center had developed, my father's reputation had grown. He had received the official title of "Yogacharya" from the equivalent of the Pope of India–known as a Shankaracharya. This allowed him to be called "yogi." But a Guru is not a title you can receive. It is something that happens naturally as the result of how people see you. Then they may begin, of their own accord, to call you a Guru. In India, Guru simply means teacher. Literally, it means one who leads from darkness to light or "one who illuminates." A guru can be an illuminator of anything, from art to dance to spirituality. They are a designated guide in a particular area of expertise. As my father began to teach from his own spiritual experience, he began to be regarded as a Guru for others on their own spiritual path.

Over the years the teachings were helping thousands of people. As programs became full and housing became tight, the center moved once again–this time to New England. I was fifteen when the center purchased an old monastery located on 250 prime acres in the heart of the New England countryside. Within a couple of years, ten thousand people per year were visiting the center. My father had come a long way from trying to scrape together enough money to buy a plane ticket and depending on the cafeteria where he worked as a busboy for food.

From being barely able to speak English, he had become an articulate and engaging orator. He became an advocate for personal introspection, looking at oneself as the source of one's own happiness or misery. He helped thousands of people release old pains, blame, and resentment of the past and move on with happier and healthier lives.

With the ensuing gratitude came hero worship. And as is often the case, as soon as we give a label to someone, we start to see them in a certain light. We begin to perceive them through an image of who we think they must be, rather than who they really are. Not only was my father perceived that way, my whole family was. The sheer immensity of what the center had become and the resultant distance between staff, program participants and us only widened that gulf; making it easy for people to decide what we must be like. In the past, when the center had been smaller, this was less of an issue. The small size meant we all had personal interactions with everyone. Everyone knew each other's faults, and took them as part of the package. Now size and distance made this less possible.

As the only daughter and the youngest, I was the little jewel in the crown. I was the little princess of a tiny little kingdom. People assumed we must be perfect; we must have the perfect family and only do "spiritual" things. They were shocked when I told them we watched TV or that my favorite food was pizza. How could this be? It didn't fit with their image of who we were.

As is the case with any daughter of a famous person, I was famous by association. Everyone wanted to be my friend. In the beginning, I trusted everyone. That was how it had been as a child and I had no reason to assume it would be different now. I told them all about me, my family, and all the things happening in our private lives. I assumed since this person was my friend, it would be kept confidential. But I soon learned, though I liked to think people genuinely liked me, there was a certain caché in being my friend. That meant anything I had repeated to them was a commodity to be traded among friends and colleagues. The closer someone was to me, the higher up they would rise in their own peer group.

Of course, everything I shared got back to my parents. They would tell me to be careful about what I said and how I acted. People listened and talked. I couldn't just freely be myself or I would get burned. I became very good at being the picture people wanted me to be. I learned to be gracious, but without showing all of who I was. I learned to listen and talk about myself without telling too much. I became a master at handling people without letting them come too close. But in the process, I had to shield a part of myself. I couldn't allow that young, child-like, exuberant self to be seen. Subtly, I learned to withdraw into a shell of polite reserve.

My father warned me. He said, as much as people loved and respected us now, they could and probably would, hate us tomorrow. He admonished me not to rely on the love and adoration people showed to him, or to me, for my sense of self worth. It could disappear in an instant. I did not learn that lesson very well, but eventually I would.

As I became an adolescent, my relationship with my father changed as well. As a child we used to be close. During his morning yoga practice I would climb all over him and we would play. I would follow him around everywhere.

But even there, distance grew as he became busy and my teenage identity kicked in. My father's own programming as an Indian dad began to take full effect. He wanted me to be a "good" Indian girl. That meant I could not go anywhere unchaperoned, not even to the mall. I was not allowed to go to friends' houses unaccompanied, or to dances with boys. I led a protected existence, effectively cut off from the rest of the world I saw going on around me. Even though I went to public school, I was not allowed to participate in anything beyond my classes. Having nothing else to do but study, I excelled.

My primary escape was through books. Books of all kinds. Mysteries. Stories of other places, other people. As I became older my taste began to gravitate towards the romance novel. My strange background, my ethnicity, and good grades practically guaranteed my lack of friends. I would walk the halls reading my book. I would cover the pain of standing alone for the bus or my solitary lunch with a book. Even if I felt alone and confined in my present life, I could read about something that had the power to lift me out of my existence. Love. Romance.

I began to believe there was something out there that could save me from feeling like this—empty and alone. I had learned from my upbringing I was the source of my own fulfillment, but I couldn't see it. It sounded good, but it was not crystal clear to me exactly how it worked. What was crystal clear was how time after time, in story after story, people (like me) found happiness when they met a partner, and that partner loved them.

I would imagine most kids have some exposure to the reality of a romantic relationship through watching their parents. Though my parents had a deep affection for one another, there was none of the romantic interaction I would expect American families had. They'd had an arranged marriage. The only thing I knew about romantic love was what I had learned in romance novels and eventually on TV. Though part of me knew what I was seeing wasn't entirely true, part of me was convinced it was a still a viable way to happiness. And that was what I wanted, to be happy.

Any Indian dad worth his salt would be an imposing father figure. My father had that plus the clout of his position. Even as his daughter, I saw him as my dad, but I also saw him as someone who was so well-respected, that to rebel against his edicts was almost unimaginable...but I did anyway.

Open defiance was not an option. So to his face, I showed him what I thought he wanted to see—the sweet, obedient Indian girl. But when my dad wasn't around, I did what I wanted. I rebelled in my own quiet way. I believed my father wanted the perfect daughter. I believed he wouldn't love me if I didn't live up to that image. So, just as I did with the people at the yoga center, I became what he wanted. Only when it was safe to do so, would I let the real me come out. In a sense it was a double-life.

Thankfully, I had some help in my corner. Shila was my second mom. She helped my mother around the house and had taken to helping with the care of us kids. She was a nanny, a best friend and a mom all rolled into one. Shila was also my chaperone. She would cover for me and let me occasionally visit my one friend after school. She helped me join the cheerleading team, my big dream, for almost an entire season before I was caught and had to quit. I even talked her into chaperoning a high school dance so I could go. Never anything too crazy, but it did give me a feeling of my own autonomy in the world. My mom knew what I was up to, but turned a blind-eye. Though tradition meant she couldn't openly go against my dad's wishes, she could pretend she knew nothing.

When she could, she would intervene on my behalf. I begged her for three years to let me take dance classes. She in turn talked to my dad, putting my case forward, until he finally said yes. It was only in these little ways that I could express a part of myself that I couldn't anywhere else in my life. I felt too confined and constrained by the role I was playing as a daughter and as the daughter of a Guru.

At school I was a nobody with almost no friends and no social life. I'd never had a date; I'd never kissed. I didn't spend any time with boys and didn't know how to act around them. I'd only slow-danced with one boy by the time I was sixteen years old. At home I was the princess, adored and cared for with many unusual opportunities and experiences, but also limited to that world. Only in small glimpses could I catch a look into the world outside my own.

CHAPTER TWO

THEN ONE DAY everything changed. I met someone who, through the glimpse he gave me of who I could be, woke me up. My entire being, my heart, came alive. Like a princess awakening from a deep sleep, I felt my savior had come to rescue me from the tower of my lonely existence. It was just like one of my favorite romance novels.

It was the first time I found myself in another's eyes. The experience was deeply heart-opening and freeing. I had longed for it for years. I thought it was the only thing that would ever make me feel that way. Since that day, and for many years after, I devoted my life to securing that feeling. Though all the teachings I had learned as a child told me this was not the way to fulfillment, my feelings and emotions were telling a different story.

At the time it was summer, and my self-appointed job was teaching Jazzercise at the yoga center. I had a few loyal students who would come and let me inexpertly lead them through a canned routine of kicks, turns and steps. I was convinced I was fabulous. My class was held in a semi-converted barn. I used a boom box as my state-of-the-art sound system. Across a calmly rippling lake, I could see the Olympic-sized outdoor swimming pool reflecting the gently rounded arches of the main building. My class didn't warrant the main building.

One day, without warning, my students just stopped coming.

"How come you're not coming to class anymore?" I asked one of them at lunch.

"There is another teacher here," she replied, as I looked into her star-struck eyes. "He is amazing. You have to meet him."

At first, I was jealous. Who was this guy taking over my classes? How dare he? Everywhere I went, I heard about him. Daren this and Daren that. "Daren is hot. Daren is in the dining room. Did you see Daren? Daren said ..." It was driving me crazy! Who was this guy, the next Messiah?

A few days later I curiously observed a gaggle of women giggling and trying to appear nonchalant as they eagerly shouldered their way past each other into the cavernous dining hall of the main building. I followed behind, and finally got my first glimpse of what, or rather who, they had been searching for. He was leaning against a table with food on it. Clearly not part of the state food code, but he had the kind of looks that would automatically exempt him from any kind of reprimand as long as the one keeping the rules was of the feminine persuasion, or gay.

From a distance his brilliant sapphire-blue eyes locked with my dark, chocolate ones. I knew it was him. It had to be. No one else could have been causing that kind of stir. I had never in my life seen anyone so handsome—or so overtly *sexy*. He looked like he'd just stepped out of one of my romance novels. Square jaw, high cheekbones, and jet-black hair paired with those blue eyes. I felt he somehow fit an inner blueprint I had unknowingly filed somewhere. Only in his being before me did I recognize he fit the blueprint to a "T". One of my former students came over to me excitedly.

"I want to introduce you to someone," she said, and began steering me in his direction. I walked towards those sapphire eyes, which never left mine. Apparently we had matching blueprints.

"I've heard a lot about you," I heard myself saying. I reached out a hand. He took it.

"I've been hearing a lot about you," he replied in a richly-resonant voice. Nice. We were still holding hands.

"Everyone has been telling me I had to meet you. You are interested in dance, right?"

"Yes," I replied. I could sense the women in our vicinity listening to our conversation as they pretended to be deeply engrossed in the couscous and salad choices in front of them. Very interesting lettuce leaves.

I dropped my hand from his, aware as always of being watched as the "daughter of ..." Anything I did or said could easily be reported back to my father, or at the very least serve as fodder for the evening gossip mill in the women's dorm.

"You should come to my class," he said. "I'd love to have you there."

"I will be there," I replied shyly. Our eyes never moved from each other. He was as taken as I was.

The next day I came to his class. I had done Jazzercise before, was somewhat coordinated, and enjoyed moving around. But that day I experienced something different. When the music came on and Daren guided us into a combination of yoga, dance and spontaneous movement, I experienced a freedom I had never known. All the inhibitions and constraints of my daily life disappeared. The real me, alive and energetic, happy and free without any cares or inhibitions, revealed herself. I sensed my own essence. The freedom there was touching and overwhelming at the same time. And to experience that opening with someone I felt such a powerful attraction to made it that much more intense. I felt he had created this opening in me and I wanted more. It was a singular experience, and truthfully was likely a major factor in my falling in love with him. He not only liked me, he had uncovered a part of me I had never known existed. He'd helped me find an inner freedom that could take me out of the limitations and inhibitions that seemed to pervade the rest of my life.

I wanted someone or something to lift me out of my constrained existence into this greater possibility. This man, I decided, could do that for me. Just like in my books.

What I didn't realize at the time was my heart did not open because of Daren, but who I allowed myself to be in his presence. I thought Daren was the source of the freedom and love I felt. I failed to recognize I *allowed* myself to go to that place when I was with him. Because of the way events came together, I *chose* to open my heart, not only to the experience, but also to the one through whom I experienced the heart opening. The way he taught helped create the environment, but he did not *make* it happen. I did. Failing to recognize this one simple fact, I attributed my feelings to him. I believed if I wanted to feel that way again, I needed *him* to make it happen. Not realizing I was the source of my own experience of love created a misplaced dependency and need.

❧

I walked out of the dining room after class and ran into Shila. I saw her as she strode towards me and I walked out to meet her, intercepting her at the edge of the swimming pool.

"I've met him," I said.

"Met who?"

"The one. I've met the love of my life and someday I will marry him," I said with absolute certainty.

Now, I have to say at this point my certainty was based on more than just a fantasy. It had a certain sense of destiny and knowing behind it, and that I cannot deny. Whether there is such a thing as past lives, soulmates, or karma—I can definitely say I felt a magnetism greater than a run-of-the-mill attraction. But what the source of the attraction is, and where destiny is meant to take us to—is up for grabs.

"What? Who? You mean Daren? Do you know how old he is? He's married!" she fired out in rapid succession. Her "mom" side was showing more than her friend side—and rightly so.

"I know," I said. "But one day I will marry him." I said it with such conviction she stopped. She knew she had to nip this in the bud before it became a problem.

"It is never going to happen," she said. "So just let it go now." I nodded my head in assent, but inside I held my wishes close to my heart.

After that day, my Jazzercise classes disappeared as if they had never been. I went to every class Daren taught. I did everything he guided us to do, following every word, every gesture, imitating his every move as if it were my own. From my perspective he was the source of my happiness, and in his presence

I felt whole. But at the same time, I could not come too close. Everyone was watching. And even if they weren't, I was too shy. It was like approaching the sun, the source of my light. What could I possibly say or do that would measure up to the intensity of feeling I had for him? Having made him my center, I was in awe. He seemed like perfection personified and I was but a lowly Cinderella who could only dream of approaching this almost unworldly, princely vision of who he was.

But like Cinderella's prince, he saw me. He was watching me, too. After class, his "groupies" would gather around, vying for his attention. He would listen and smile. Slowly, as if by chance, his blue-eyed gaze would wander over to where I was gathering my things at the back of the room. Feeling the weight of his glance, I could feel my body begin to radiate like a heating coil without even looking at him. I would let my gaze catch his—ever so slightly—the intensity so great I could hardly hold his glance for more than a fraction of a moment.

Because of my position, everything I did, every move I made, and every glance to Daren was closely watched. Though I was convinced I was playing my cards close to my chest, I'm sure my feelings gave me away. But nothing was said, and there were no repercussions. I was safe for the moment.

That summer, having challenges with my teenage plumpness, I began to lose weight almost overnight. I would "happen" to be washing a car in a t-shirt and shorts as he walked into the back entrance of the building. There was some piece of music I just "knew" he'd want to have. The smallest contact took on the greatest significance. It was as if I lived in a dream-like world that revolved around one person—everything else taking second place to the central theme of my life—Daren.

CHAPTER THREE

S UMMER TURNED TO FALL, and it was time to go back to school. I submitted once again to the confines of my life. But the one thing I could use to free my consciousness, besides my books, was the memory of "him." He was the embodiment of the heart opening I experienced. I held the memory of that completeness strongly in my mind. I used it to motivate myself. I looked forward to the next summer when I would see him; the memory of how it was, and the anticipation of how it would be, kept me going. I lost more weight. I got into shape. I was looking forward to showing off my "new" self to Daren. I unconsciously hoped my new image would somehow bring me closer to the completeness I associated with him.

Summer came again. My anticipation grew. I had signed up for dance training with Daren at the center. My fantasy, carefully fed each day, had grown through the course of time. I was in a state of perpetual excitement at the thought of seeing him again. It was a way to keep myself thinking about a happy future in order to deal with my present life. But I was so wrapped up in the future I was robbing myself of the one place I might have found contentment—right now. While a future fantasy might make the present appear more palatable for a time, it could never provide the same level of fulfillment a real-life present moment experience could—just as a mirage can never fulfill one's thirst like a true glass of water.

In this heightened state of expectancy, I spent the afternoon carefully preparing myself for our opening session. I had to dress so I looked my best, without appearing I was making an effort. I tried on and discarded combination upon combination of leotards, sweatpants, t-shirts and tank tops until they were piled on every available surface of my bedroom. Which one would do it? Which one would most likely get me the outcome

I was looking for—the fairytale ending to my fantasy? Which lipstick, which eyeliner, which hairdo would get him to look at me the way he had done the very first time he met me? If I could just find the right combination of ingredients I could make it happen again. And if I could reproduce it, I could feel that way again.

LOOKING GOOD

Sometimes women spend time on their clothes, hair and makeup because it empowers them. It helps remind them, in a concrete way, how beautiful they are. It is a way to express what is within to the outside world. At other times the outfit, the look, the eyes, are all designed for one thing–to create the external validation that will help fill an imaginary sense of lack.

For me, it was the latter. I wanted to look my most beautiful, because by looking my best I could increase my chances of getting Daren's attention. And if I got his attention, I would get love. And if I got love, I would feel okay. I would feel beautiful enough to deserve love. Spending hours agonizing over outfits, hair and makeup was a small price to pay to get such a big return it seemed.

With hopeful eagerness to see Daren again, I walked into the auditorium. A group of about 50 men and women were circled at the front of the room. I strained to see Daren's face among them. I couldn't see him. My heart was beating in my throat, my breath shallow. Where was he? Could he see me? Was he looking at me now? I was waiting for the moment our eyes would once again meet and I would feel the feeling I had waited for all winter.

I approached the group, continuing to unobtrusively scan the group for his face. Was he in the bathroom? Had he not yet arrived? I sat down with the rest of the group, trying not to look disturbed.

Carolyn, a diminutive blond with a wide, toothy smile was calmly leading the opening introduction. No mention of Daren was made. What was happening? Where was my storybook?

I was so lost in my speculative thoughts I didn't hear what Carolyn was saying until Daren's name was mentioned.

"… and he won't be arriving for another ten days, if at all," she said.

What?!!!! But I had waited all winter. I had worked out, dreamed, imagined, and fantasized about the moment when he would turn to me with desire-filled eyes, and now he might not be coming at all? This was not a pleasant surprise by any stretch of the imagination.

Suddenly, my source of happiness had been taken from me. The way I had felt in the dance. The connection to myself. The promising excitement of dancing with Daren, the daydreams I'd created running through every gesture, glance and word with Daren slipped away. Now that I believed Daren was the source of the wholeness I had felt, it seemed I could not feel that way without him. I mistook him to be my source and in doing so gave myself away.

Now, without Daren, I was just left with a month of dance training. Just this. Just me. No one else. *Boooriiing!!!* In comparison to the expectations I had built up in my head, real life just didn't measure up. No matter that people paid thousands of dollars and saved for years for the kind of training I was about to do for free. I could not appreciate what was in front of me because I believed only Daren could make me feel the way I wanted to. Without him I couldn't be fulfilled. And because I believed it to be true, that is how it was.

This was the first time of many that I began to glimpse something it took me years to fully assimilate. Once I decided someone else was the source of my happiness, I had to possess their attention. The way society had taught me to get it was to tie myself up in knots trying to find the best hair, makeup, clothes, body and personality, all so I could get this one person to look at me in a certain way, so I could feel whole. But this path to wholeness was not the best way to feel good about myself. In fact, it felt terrible, though I didn't fully notice it at the time. I never seemed to be able to be pretty enough, thin enough, or nice enough. I had my own inner ideal of how I had to be to be lovable, and until that picture was fulfilled, I was convinced I wouldn't get the love I so wanted. Twenty pounds was not enough. Every curve, every bump seemed to taunt me. *You are not good enough. He will never love you the way you are. You have to be different.*

PRINCE CHARMING

My theory on love is this: from a very young age, we receive all kinds of impressions that help us develop a sense of who we are. Based on this adopted collection of ideas, thoughts, and opinions, we formulate an image of happiness as well as an image of the kind of person we believe can make us happy.

Our image of happiness is usually in compensation for, or an attempt to reproduce, what we experienced in the past. Or it may be based on accomplishing a social ideal. We may try to be happy by striving to replicate society's image of accomplishment, beauty, or intelligence. We may seek it by replicating a pleasurable experience from the past or avoiding an unpleasant one. Or, perhaps we try to make up for an unhappy past with the promise of a brighter future.

Similarly, based on our accumulated history, we tend to search for one of four things from a partner:

1. *We try to find a partner that fits a socially recognized ideal.*

2. *We look for a partner that helps us replicate a pleasurable experience from the past.*

3. *We seek out a partner who will not cause us to re-experience an unpleasant event.*

4. *We look for someone who will make up for a painful event from the past.*

After all, who is our imagined perfect partner? Isn't it someone who at least in some ways fits cultural norms like having a job, being a good provider, or a good parent? Isn't it someone who *isn't* like the people who hurt us in the past? Someone who will make up for our pain, or who reminds us of someone who nurtured and cared for us? Isn't it also someone who possesses some key structural elements that match our psyche? Let me state there is nothing wrong with this. It is perfectly natural and makes logical sense. Where we get caught is when what we would *like* is confused with what we *need* to be happy.

We carry this picture around and it already exists before anyone out there even shows up. Unconsciously, we "match" our picture to everyone we meet. Does this person fit my picture? Does that one?

I have come to believe at least part of the "love at first sight" experience we have is a function of the inner blueprint we carry. As a result of that fit, we open up. Certain ingredients we have been searching for come together. In the presence of those ingredients, it is effortless for our heart to be open to this person. This powerful and spontaneous triggering of heart-opening is what we call love. Our capacity to embrace the other just as they are is natural, spontaneous and effortless. It spills over to everyone in our vicinity. Because our heart happens to open in the presence of this person, it appears that they are "doing" it. We attribute the love we feel to them, and they become our prince or princess "charming." Because we think they are the cause of our heart opening, we become dependent on them to continually give us this feeling.

Daren was definitely my prince charming. He had all the ingredients my inner blueprint seemed to require. Certainly I saw him as an antidote to the restrictions I felt. Not only that, he was startlingly handsome and charismatic, everyone wanted him, and he wanted me. And, last but not least, he was just out of my reach. No prince charming is nearly as interesting if we can have him right away. The longing for the unattainable was undeniable. It set up a yearning in me to have that thing—the promise of my fantasy fulfilled. It gave my life a sort of romantic rosiness, a vision of wholeness. The problem was until that fantasy was realized; my life would always, after a few moments, days or weeks of contentment, return to feeling just a little bit incomplete.

To me these are the ingredients that make for romantic love: the picture, the person who seems to fit the picture, the longing, and hopefully, the resolution. And if we think about it, these are the exact ingredients that make up any good romance novel.

Then and there Daren became the source of my longing. He was my inroad to the expansive experience of all-encompassing wholeness. In much the same way as the Juliets of the past pined over their Romeos, I decided that someday Daren would be mine. And with that romantic resolution, my life would be complete. I would live happily ever after and that would be that. Easy.

As the years passed, my infatuation with my personified ideal continued. Every year we would run into each other. Every year the intensity of the attraction was equally strong. But our attraction for each other had been noticed. People were always around making sure that nothing untoward could happen. Even the smallest stolen glance or touch took on significance. Once, standing outside the auditorium where he would teach, he was stretching out his leg on a bar as a ballet dancer might do. Without thinking, I reached out and took his foot. The moment my hand touched his foot, I felt an electric exchange. My gaze reached his, for once, devoid of any shyness. The intensity of feeling was palpable, but no words were spoken. Too many people were around.

Later that day, one of the women who organized Daren's visits to the center came up to me.

"Your attraction for Daren is obvious," she ground out. "If you keep it up, you will ruin it for all of us and I'm not going to let that happen." With that, I was more or less ordered to keep my distance.

My interactions with Daren were further reduced to a series of hopeful chance encounters over summer vacations and holidays. Each time, I would roam the hallways hoping to run into him; going to every place he might be while wearing my best. Rarely were we ever able to exchange more than a sentence. But the memory of that first experience of love kept me going when sense should have told me to move on.

One fateful day, now eighteen years old, I decided to take a chance. Having found out Daren was staying on the fourth floor, I camped out in Shila's room—also conveniently located on the fourth floor. I left the door open so should he walk by, he would *happen* to see me. What machinations we are willing to go through for love! Sure enough, after a seemingly interminable span of time, he walked by. He saw me. I had a present for him. A sweater. It didn't fit, but endearingly, he left it on anyway.

"I was thinking about taking a walk tomorrow morning," I said carefully.

"Oh really?" he smiled.

"Yes, I'm thinking of going down to the lake at around nine o'clock." I looked at him invitingly, but said nothing further. He had to make the next move.

"I think that is a good idea. I'll meet you in the lobby," he said, obligingly filling in his lines.

I was overjoyed with his reply and could hardly sleep that night. My mind went through every possible scenario. What would he say? What would I say? What should I wear? Maybe we would be able to hold hands or, the unthinkable of the unthinkable, we might kiss. Daren was separated now, so it *was* a possibility I told myself. I tried to imagine what it would feel like and found I could reproduce it perfectly in my mind. The touch, the electric exchange, the drumming of my heart as our lips touched. In my mind I could manipulate the scenario to go exactly the way I wanted. Whether real-life was going to cooperate was another story.

That morning, I dressed carefully. By now, I had perfected the art of looking like I hadn't tried to look good. I believe the magazines call it "the natural look." I am aware that a true natural look would have consisted of getting out of bed and washing my face. My version was trying to look as if I accidentally fell out of bed with subtly tinted lips, mascara and just a hint of shadow highlighting my eyes. The hair was mussed to look just a little windblown, but my hair hadn't seen any wind since the day before.

Satisfied with my reflection, I made my way downstairs. He was waiting, his back turned away from me as he took in the intense colors of the autumn leaves. Sensing my presence, he turned and smiled. My heart was pounding not only with excitement, but also with fear.

I knew what I was about to do was *soooo* against my father's rules. I had never dared do anything so overtly contrary to his wishes. And worse still, people would inevitably see us. But in my quest to experience that feeling (you know the one), I bore on.

We walked slowly down the massive stone steps and down the gently descending hill on which the main building rested. At first, our conversation was stilted. Then, as we moved out of view of the main building, and watchful eyes, I relaxed. Daren, seemingly unaware of my inner turmoil, cheerily chatted on. But as we entered the woods, he was careful to keep a polite distance and did not take my hand. He knew we were in uncertain territory as well. Nevertheless, our proximity to each other worked its magic. I felt a thrill of anticipation move through me. We sat at the lake for a while.

I told Daren about feeling confined in my life as the teenage daughter of a father who wanted me to keep to Indian traditions. As we made our way back through the woods and up the hill, I felt I had gotten what I wanted. This was the longest we had ever spoken, the most private contact we'd ever had. Now all that was left was the price I would have to pay for it. I half-hoped that nothing would happen. After all, 350 people lived and worked at the center.

"Who could possibly be interested in what I was doing?" I told myself. As we crested the last hillock, a figure came running towards us.

Trying to catch her breath the figure, a woman whose name I have since forgotten panted out, "Your father is looking for you. He wants you to call him right away."

I had my answer. There would be no reprieve.

Daren strode ahead of me. "I'll talk to him," he said, full of resolve.

"No," I replied. "I have to do this."

We turned to go into the main entrance, still a good distance away, but the white-clad messenger spoke urgently. "He wants to speak to you right away. You'd better go in the west-side entrance."

I turned and said goodbye to Daren. I felt to stay together would only be more damning. My heart heavy, I trudged the last steps to the west-entrance of the building. I dialed the phone and my father picked up on the first ring.

"Where have you been?" he said. Of course he knew very well where I had been. But some part of me was holding out hope against hope he was calling me for some other reason.

I replied as nonchalantly as possible, "I went for a walk."

"Alone?"

"No, with people."

"People? Who was with you?"

"Ed …. and Daren was there, too," I said, desperately grasping at straws. Of course Ed had not been there as would have been plain for anyone to see. What is it about confrontation that makes us try to cover up even in the face of irrefutable evidence?

"Daren? You went for a walk with Daren and Ed? Are you sure?" he asked. This was excruciating! How had I gotten myself into this mess? Where was my courage?

"No," I replied softly. "I'm not sure." Of course he had known the truth all along and was testing me out. Clearly I had not passed the test by any stretch of the imagination, and believe me, I can stretch very far.

"Come up to the house immediately."

With resignation, I hung up the phone and reluctantly made my way up towards the house. I searched the building for any sign of Daren, but did not see him anywhere. Upon arrival, I was ushered into my father's meeting room. Not good.

"How can I ask people to follow the rules when my own daughter doesn't listen to me?" my father asked, in all sincerity.

I had heard different versions of this theme since I was a child. I knew it by heart. For Caesar it had been "Veni, vidi, vici." For France it was liberté, égalité, fraternité. For the United States it was "E pluribus unum." For me it was, "Your life should be an example to others." I mumbled along in agreement to my father's words and humbly nodded my head at the requisite moments. Finally, I was allowed to go. I had long ago learned not to speak up. Speaking up was dangerous. Better to shut my mouth and stay quiet. It just seemed to make things easier on everyone.

Defeated, I walked up to my room and snuggled deep under the covers. I wanted to disappear. And for a time I found forgetfulness in sleep. When I woke up, I dressed and went down to the main building.

Daren was there. I approached, but kept my distance. No need to incur the wrath of the gods (or in this case my dad) two times in one day! Daren said he and my father had spoken. Not one word was exchanged about our walk or Daren's connection to me. Just conversation. "What are you up to? How is your business doing?" That kind of thing. Nothing else. But apparently no direct words were necessary. Daren had his bags next to him. He was leaving posthaste. He deliberately caught my eyes and told me what could not be said in words. He was sorry and sad. But this was more than he was prepared for. His respect for my father was too great to go against him. And I understood. I couldn't either.

Daren rarely came to the center after that. And when he did, it was while I was away at school.

CHAPTER FOUR

THE MEMORY OF DAREN faded, though never completely disappeared. I went off to Smith College and had my own new adventures there. My ever-protective father allowed me to live on-campus, but only because it was a respected women's college.

The year I graduated, I was invited to Toronto to assist an organizational consultant. Finally, I was of age, Daren was single, and he was living in Toronto. The gap in our ages didn't seem to matter as much now as it did when I was younger. I stayed with my friend Sita, a Canadian of Guyanese/Indian descent, who had always acted as a sort of go-between at the center for Daren and me. She would be the "chaperone" so that we could sometimes have a moment in relative privacy.

Heading up to Toronto made me think about Daren all the more. As stress and boredom during the ten-hour drive escalated, my fantasies began to run rampant. But even then I felt I had a lot more confidence and a lot less energy invested in him than before. I was ambivalent, and maybe even a little apprehensive. Even if I did manage to see him, would the electrical current once so strong between us still be there? And if it wasn't, what would I do? If it was, how was I supposed to act? I was free now, but what did I really want to happen? Only one way to find out. Not even my current anxieties were going to stop me from what I had wanted for so long.

Sita gave me his number and I called him. The first time, my heart was beating fast. A boy answered. Daren was not home. The second time I called a girl answered. She said he wasn't there, but this time I left a message with my telephone number. I put down the phone and was walking towards my bedroom when the phone rang. Sita picked up the phone. It was him. She handed me the phone.

"Hello my Indian princess, this is your Daren," he rolled out smoothly. That rich, resonant voice at once melted my insides and made my heart jump into my throat. But at the same time, age and distance had lessened my need for him, and he sounded just a little less sexy. Unfortunately, that composure did not extend to my communication skills.

"Hi!" I managed to stumble out. I winced as I said it.

"So you're in Toronto," he said after waiting for what seemed an interminable about of time.

"Yes." Oh, I was on a roll now! A whole word spoken without stuttering!

"The girl you spoke with on the phone is my niece. She came out to me in the garden and said, 'Do you know anyone named Ka-mini?'"

"Kamini?!" he had asked. He was shocked and couldn't believe it was possible.

"Yeah, I thought you'd be surprised," I replied coolly. I was starting to find my "confident" twenty-two year-old persona.

"How did you get up here?"

"I have a car now. I'm old."

"I'm the one who's old," he said and laughed.

He asked how long I'd been away from home and I said four years. That I'd been at Smith and had just graduated with high honors in Anthropology and Sociology. He asked what I was doing here and I told him I was assisting at a consulting firm.

"Maybe we should see each other. Maybe Sita would like to come too," he said.

"That would be great," I replied. Though part of me had hoped it would be just the two of us, I didn't know if I could handle being completely alone with him. Sita would be a good buffer. I managed to get out the details and we agreed that the three of us would meet up after my workday the following afternoon.

The next day I was filled with anticipation, but also fear. Plans had gone awry before. Would it work out this time? When

I walked into the lobby, would he be there? Finally the appointed hour came. I wrapped up my duties as quickly as I could and made small talk as I walked with some of the staff to the lobby. I subtly scanned the room for a sign of him. Then I scanned a little less subtly.

"Are you looking for someone?" a colleague asked. My co-workers and boss knew Daren, and they also knew something about our past attraction.

"Oh, just a friend who was going to meet me," I replied in the most casual tone I could muster. Why had I not thought of this? If Daren actually did show up, they would all see him! And if they did see him, chances were that this juicy tidbit would wind its way back to my father.

I calmed myself. "I'm grown up now," I said to myself. "It doesn't matter what my dad thinks or says." Riiiight.

But it was all a moot point anyway. Daren was nowhere in sight. I lingered for thirty minutes. I glanced over at Sita a few times. We looked at each other and shrugged philosophically. He wasn't coming. I was okay with this. Though I had my hopes and fantasies, I knew that the chances of us ever having any kind of real relationship were slim to none. More than anything, I wanted closure so I wouldn't always have this dream of being with him in the back of my mind. If it wasn't going to happen, I wanted to let it go completely. I took it as a sign that the time for letting go had come.

I walked down the stairs with my boss and colleagues. Suddenly, there he was at the foot of the stairs, his lean, sinewy frame propped against the wall. As he saw me, he slowly smiled and turned to face me. My heart leapt in my throat. I wanted to return the smile in full wattage, but was foiled by my colleagues who were now very attentive to the fact that some juicy gossip was in the making. Trying to keep my cool as best as I could, I approached. Sita had already passed him and said she'd see us in the parking lot. The others nodded to Daren as they walked by, a couple even threw knowing glances at me. I turned back to

Daren. As the last faces disappeared around the corner Daren and I started to laugh.

"Some things never change," he laughed. I agreed. He loved to laugh like me.

He held out his hand, and I took it. The electricity was there in spades, and all thoughts of "completion and moving on" disappeared as if they had never been.

Daren and I drove to an Indian restaurant we had agreed upon earlier. Sita followed. In the space of silence that filled the car, I spilled everything; living in Switzerland, my first boyfriend whom I'd met there, my dad. He said I was as beautiful as always. That my hair had grown and he liked it. He asked if he looked any different. I thought he seemed shorter, but I didn't tell him that. I had built him up so much in my mind he just appeared shorter than the picture I had of him. But he looked as fantastic as I remembered.

The three of us sat down and ordered. Daren had been divorced a year before. He was open about his breakup and his concern for his children. Yes, children. Three to be exact. Before the meal was served Sita stood and took her leave. She was very diplomatic and neither of us demurred.

The first few moments after she left, I was nervous. My heart was beating so fast, I wanted to run away.

Instead, I smiled and said jauntily, "Well, that was well executed, don't you think?"

"Yes," he said. "Did she do it on purpose?" Men. Sometimes they just don't get it. So I said to him, "She told me she would need to leave early." No need to get into a treatise on female machinations.

We talked about many things. I learned he had been a gymnast, a piano player, a fine artist and an actor. He talked about his young years and how he had become a draw for so many people.

I was honest with him about the challenges I faced with my father and my own self-expression.

Finally, our conversation fell silent. I could feel the words forming in my mouth, and I wasn't sure if I should hold them back or not. Perhaps I should tell the truth. It might be the only time we ever had to be together.

Bracing myself with a deep breath I stumbled out, "I have dated one or two men now and it has been fun. I'm glad I finally got a chance to get out there and have some experience of the world." As the next words came my throat tightened and I had to clear my throat to get out the next sentence, "But I've never felt with any of them what I felt with you–even though nothing ever happened between us." Coughing, I reached out, took a sip of water, staring at my glass. I had bared my most vulnerable feelings and couldn't look up.

Within my line of vision came Daren's hand to rest on mine. "I love you too, Kamini." For a time we were both silent. Now, a possibility for us existed which had never been there before. Everything we said and did was no longer a game. It was real and there would be consequences. Both of us realized this and in that moment recognized the enormity of what we might be opening ourselves up to.

At around 10pm or so Daren was anxious to leave. We walked to the car hand-in-hand. It was an amazing feeling to be able to do this with impunity. We drove in relative silence to Sita's home, only occasionally breaking the silence with a comment here or there. Daren was clearly deep in thought. As we pulled up to the driveway, he stopped the car.

Visibly uncertain, he said, "I'd like to take you out and just have some time to explore who we are together. Would that be all right?" All right? All right? Are you kidding me? This was my dream coming true!

"Sure," I replied. We talked a little more, and agreed that after my work I would stay on for a week. I undid my seatbelt, wondering if he would kiss me. Instead, he leaned over and hugged me. It didn't quite fit my picture, but since the rest was so mind-blowing, I was willing to let it go for the moment.

That night I was over the moon with the turn of events. I could not believe what had happened all in one night. But my mind still kept on coming back to the one thing that had not gone according to my expectations. The kiss. Why had he hugged me and not kissed me? Just hours before, I would have been delighted to get a hug from Daren. But my imagination had created a more perfect reality than this one could match. Even with everything I had hoped for on the brink of materializing, all I could think about was what was missing. Not really missing, but missing because I had already attached to a picture of how it could have been—what could have made it more perfect and romantic. Even though I had more, I somehow felt I had less. The comparison thing again.

Over the next week, we existed in a dream bubble. We went to Ontario place, we went dancing, I went to his exercise class at King Ranch, and we went to his niece's school concert.

Before the concert we talked about us. About how my father would feel about all this. It started to become real, and the more real it became, the more I began to feel divided. On the one hand, I was terrified. This news would be a huge scandal. My father would never allow it. And even in my besotted state, I was aware that a divorce, combined with three kids and a substantial age difference, could be a disaster in the making. I was only twenty-two after all...barely beginning my life. He was thirty-five.

But on the other hand, the attraction I felt was so intense, my love so strong, I could imagine a scenario in which all those obstacles could be overcome. At least that's what I told myself. In my desire to make my dream come true, I was willing to overlook all signs of reality.

On our last morning, we agreed to write, call, and visit when possible. We would let things develop over time and see where it went. I knew that Daren was not the most dependable guy, but I wanted to give it a chance to happen. If he didn't call or write I would be able to say I had followed it to its natural completion. If he did, it would be a welcome surprise and we would see where things went.

On the ten-hour drive home, I thought about us. How would I tell all this to my father? What would the fallout be? I couldn't even imagine telling him. But then I would bring the memory of Daren to mind. I could conjure the feeling I had when I was with him, and my courage came back to me. I spent ten hours like this, going back and forth with no resolution in sight.

I got home and only my brother was there. I told him I had seen Daren and he wanted to have a relationship with me.

"Are you crazy?" he said, his tone shocked. "He's divorced. He has three kids. You are twenty-two years old. He has the reputation as a bit of a playboy. Do you think dad is going to be okay with that? He will never allow it. And you are only going to get hurt by him. Get on the phone and call Daren now. Tell him you changed your mind."

Here was the dose of reality I had so assiduously avoided. My romantic fabrications dropped with a thud back to earth. Suddenly I did not feel very well. I went to my room to lick my wounds.

I didn't call Daren. And I didn't tell my father either. I decided to see how things developed between us first, before I tested the waters with my dad. No need to muddy things until absolutely necessary. Maybe there was still hope to make this whole thing produce the outcome I so dearly wanted–the love, admiration, and fulfillment to quiet that place in me that always felt not good enough.

I faithfully wrote letters to Daren, but received no reply. I called and left messages, but never got a response. At first, I made excuses; he was busy with his new job, finding a place to live, etc, etc... but at some point, it was patently clear that nothing was happening.

By now, four months had passed. I was working on a project to assist at a wellness week in Italy, followed by a weekend seminar with my dad. I was busy helping with the promotion of the project—writing copy and getting the information distributed to our European contacts. I felt fulfilled and took pride in having a project through which I could express my creative energies.

The more I found satisfaction through my own self-expression, the less I found myself concerned with Daren and what he was or was not doing. I did not need the fantasy of him to make me feel better. I felt good about myself. I was filled with my own sense of self-worth and didn't need someone else to give it to me. It felt good, and it felt right.

I picked up the phone and called him. It was the first time I reached him in person, and ironic that the most real conversation we ever had was the one in which I broke it off.

I told him I took that he had not called or written to mean he was no longer interested. Not true, he protested. He had been very busy, but had been thinking a lot about me. The issue for him was that I was not willing to tell my father the truth. It was hard enough to have a long distance relationship he said without compounding it with sneaking around and dishonesty. He had a solid point. But in the end, I did not have the courage to tell my father the truth and face his disappointment. So we agreed we would always love one another, but things would end here.

Strangely, I was not as disappointed as I would have imagined. It was clear to me in that moment the path to fulfillment was through devotion to my own full self-expression. Whether it was work, love, or anything else, if it was an expression of me, it would be fruitful and deeply fulfilling. If, on the other hand, it were used as a way to validate my worth, I would never find the lasting wholeness I was seeking. So, at the age of 22, I made a choice. I made the choice to find my expression through teaching, developing my career, traveling and the full enjoyment of my life and its possibilities. It was a wonderful, empowering time. It lasted for a total of 25 days.

CHAPTER FIVE

THREE WEEKS AFTER our breakup, I was on a plane to Italy for the wellness week. A team of us traveled together to put on the weeklong program, and I was but a lowly assistant. It was September when we arrived at a ski lodge in the Italian Dolomites, in the mountain town of Marilleva. Off-season, the lodge was virtually empty, all but for us. Large and cavernous, we explored room after room from the indoor theater, to the sauna, pool and disco. The usually snow-covered slopes were replaced with majestic views of grassy inclines, summer flowers, and the town of Trento below.

Though the start was slow and painstaking, in short order we were all occupied with our tasks: setting up registration, the program room, typing up schedules, making signs and name-tags. At meals we would all sit together, discuss our progress and enjoy the culinary delights the Italian chef had created for us.

At lunch on registration day, two of my colleagues came to tell me the first registrant had arrived.

Knowing my penchant for handsome men, one said, "You'd better hurry. It could be your future husband out there." I laughed. I was no longer interested in getting serious about a man, but I thought it was funny anyway.

I walked out to the front desk and saw him–dirty blond hair, six foot two, square jaw, high cheekbones and slanting, leonine green eyes. Definitely my cup of tea. But this man was not only handsome, he was radiant. He glowed. His smile was boyishly shy and charming. I was mesmerized, and I knew with a certainty he would be very important in my life.

I nervously went about checking him in. His name was Steve and he was from the Netherlands. As the first to arrive, I took it upon myself to show him to his room. The polite thing for a hostess to do after all!

That night as members introduced themselves, the program leader urged me to join an odd-numbered group and talk to Steve. He had come on the advice of his sister, Marjan, whom I knew from programs I had assisted in the Netherlands. Though I had invited her, it was Steve who was looking for spiritual direction. "I have just the thing for you," she'd told him. He got on a train to Italy to attend the workshop with no idea what to expect or even why he was there. He'd simply felt drawn to come.

SLIPPING BACK INTO OLD PATTERNS

In the month since the breakup with Daren, I'd had a glimpse of finding fulfillment through my own self-expression in the world. But my overwhelming programming, my default-behavior, was to seek wholeness through the external, everything outside myself. Steve showed up, and all thoughts of "self-fulfillment" evaporated. Twenty-five days could not stand up to a lifetime of programming. It was not even a choice. The option to stay rooted in myself as I began to relate to him did not even arise. Everything went out the window in the face of the remembered pleasure of finding love through another. And because society recognized this as a valid method for finding what I was looking for, the tendency to allow this programming to run its course was even greater. There was no counter-force to mitigate the overwhelming desire to find wholeness by losing myself in a relationship.

Finding wholeness through relationship is not bad in itself, but the distinction was this: In seeking wholeness, was I finding myself in the relationship, or losing myself in it? Did I know I was okay whether I was in a relationship or not? Or was I dependant on it to feel okay? For me, at that time, it was the latter on both counts. No holds barred. There was no real consideration given to any other option. That was what romance novels had taught me, my experience had reinforced, and what my past experience led me to try to replicate in the present moment. Just because it hadn't turned out the way I wanted with Daren didn't mean I couldn't make it happen with Steve. All I had to do was reproduce the great things I had with Daren and avoid all the things that didn't work about us...and voila! I'd have a perfect relationship ready to fulfill me for the rest of my life.

Once again, I embarked on the very tenuous journey of trying to make my storybook happen. What I found was real people do not play the characters we construct for them very well. What an uncertain existence to be completely at the effect of someone else's changing whims to feel good!

After the first morning yoga class that week, I stayed behind to clean up the room. Steve stayed on to practice Tai Chi. Over the next couple of days he would practice while I cleaned up, and then teach me a few moves before we headed down to breakfast together. Though we shared this little bit of time and sat near each other at meals, there was little further contact.

One morning as we left the yoga room, the teacher asked who would be joining the optional group excursion the following day. I raised my hand along with most of the others until I saw that Steve had not raised his hand. I quickly lowered my hand hoping he hadn't seen. (I later found out he had). Whatever he was doing was what I wanted to be doing.

As we walked out of the room that day after our usual Tai Chi lesson, I casually asked, "Are you going on the trip to town today?"

"No," he replied. Of course I already knew the answer.

Knowing he enjoyed hiking and had been walking in the mountains the day before I said, "I'm not going either. I'm thinking of going hiking. What are you going to do?"

"I was thinking of going up to a mountain lake I heard about."

"Oh," I said, feigning surprise at this happy coincidence. "Maybe we can go together?"

With that planned, we made our way down to breakfast. I was sparkling. Things were going my way!

The conversation made its way to discussion of the disco. Several others and I made a plan to go that evening. Steve said nothing, but if he were interested he would know where I was.

That night, I was exhausted. After all, I was also assisting in the workshop all the while. Though truthfully, it felt more like I was falling in love, with a workshop in the background. I decided to skip the disco. I got into bed and turned out the light, but I couldn't sleep. What if Steve was there? I would be passing up an opportunity. Maybe THE opportunity.

Suddenly, tiredness gone, I jumped out of bed. In less than ten minutes I was dressed and on my way down to the disco. Sure enough our group was there. So was Steve. I was elated. Dancing was my thing. In the beginning we all danced together as a group. Then it thinned out until it was just a few of us. Steve and I danced quite a bit together. We had a great time and he impressed me with his moves. But then he did something that was definitely not part of the plan. He started dancing with another girl!

Now, having given my sense of self completely over to what was happening in our developing relationship, I had no ground to stand on when that was taken away. I went from ecstatic to crushed in a matter of seconds. All the air went out of my artificially inflated sense of self. I was back to me. And even worse, having abandoned myself, I no longer had a strong center to come back to.

We continued to dance with one another intermittently throughout the evening, but now Mika, the girl he was dancing with, became my rival. She became the source of the pain I was experiencing, and an obstacle to the solution. But only because I had decided having Steve was the solution. All I had to do was get him to pay attention to me over her and I could have that feeling back. If I hadn't needed his attentions to feel good, she would not have appeared as a problem.

We danced into the early hours, and up to the end, I did not know if Steve had chosen Mika or me. My sense of self was completely reliant on his choice. That night, I won out. Steve offered to walk me to my room. He gave me the customary European kiss on each cheek. The mutual attraction was clear, and I was not giving up on my solution.

WE GET TO KNOW THE OTHER
BY BEING SOMEONE WE'RE NOT

When we first meet someone, we don't tend to present who we are. We present who we *think* we should be. A big part of that is constructed from what we think the other person will find attractive. So here we are, looking for someone who we can be ourselves with, but we don't show them fully who we are.

This became apparent to me the next day. Steve and I met in the lobby for our hike. He had a backpack all ready with water and a little picnic for us. I thought it was romantic. He had done his bit to please me. For him I was walking up a mountain, when I have no interest in hiking. It is uncomfortable, it makes me sweat, and because I rarely do it, I have to exert a lot of will not to appear as if I'm about to keel over from a heart attack. However, this was what Steve liked to do and I was going to do it with him. It was how I could plausibly spend time with him and impress upon him the myriad ways in which we were infinitely compatible with each other.

I was wearing my cutest jeans—which molded to my rounded hips, and held in my tummy to perfection. My hair was neatly braided and casually thrown over one shoulder. I wore a red t-shirt to highlight my golden complexion and dark eyes. A jaunty little red and white Italian scarf wrapped around my neck, I was ready to impress.

The first few hundred feet were not so bad. I could actually talk to Steve in a normal tone of voice. This is going well, I thought. We'll walk like this for an hour tops, then sit down and have a leisurely picnic by the lake. My fantasy lasted until we started climbing in earnest. This was not the hiking I had done in the mountains of New England. These were the Italian Alps with genuinely steep trails! And, I'd forgotten about altitude! Any fitness I did have would be further compromised by the ability of my body to absorb oxygen at this height. All I could hope was the mountain lake was not far away. Neither Steve nor I knew the exact distance.

The trail rose ahead of us step after step, turn after turn. The jeans that had once felt so endearingly formfitting now inhibited my every step. I could feel my lungs struggling to take in air. I desperately wanted to gasp to be able to keep going, but that option was ruled out. Heavy breathing in front of men I'm interested in is not a good look for me.

Steve, suddenly feeling completely at ease in the midst of my seemingly incredible listening skills, continued to chatter on, telling me about his life, his relationships and what brought him to the workshop. But his voice was background noise. All I could focus on was breathing in and breathing out without wheezing, putting one foot in front of the other with legs that were threatening to collapse under me at any minute. Why was I doing this again? Ah yes, love. And getting love meant impressing the person who could give it to me.

"Are you okay?" he asked, breaking into my reverie.

"Yes, I'm fine," I managed to get out before needing to catch my next breath. Breathing in the middle of a sentence is a dead giveaway. I stopped and pretended to take in the scenery. I willed my heart to slow down, my breath to become even.

"Beautiful view isn't it? I enjoy taking my time and enjoying the landscape as it unfolds," I said.

Lie! Big lie! Even now, I could only partially take in what was in front of me. I was completely preoccupied with trying to stay upright and look as if this was an enjoyable jaunt in the woods. What I was really trying to say was, "I'm exhausted, and I don't think I can go any further without taking breaks at five minute intervals." But did I say that? No way. That would blow the picture I was carefully trying to construct.

Three hours and many stops to "enjoy the view" later, we finally made it to the lake. My legs were trembling uncontrollably; my red and white scarf was dark with sweat. But I had made it!

The lake was stunningly beautiful. Just like those pictures you see of mountain lakes. Flowers still in bloom. Green meadows and mountains rising on all sides. Not a single soul to be seen but us. This was what I had suffered for.

We walked halfway around the lake and then stopped to put our feet in. I was covered with sweat and desperately needed to cool off. I also thought it would be very adventurous and spontaneous if I suggested we go in the lake. Steve had his bathing trunks. I put his t-shirt on over my underwear and went in headfirst. It was glacial. I could hardly take a full breath. In the time it took to talk Steve into the water, my whole body had gone numb. I suddenly felt my leg begin to cramp up. I didn't say anything but suggested we go back to shore.

We sat in the sun to dry out, still frigid with cold and without a towel. Steve warmed me up as best as he could, and we sat in companionable silence. I felt comfortable. I felt I could be myself. Though, if that was the case, I'm not sure why I needed to go through my whole charade. Nevertheless, I settled back and began to enjoy the fruits of my labor in earnest. I felt all my struggles had been worth this reward.

As we began to set up for our picnic, my muscles began to involuntarily cramp up. First it was my feet. I tried to stretch them out, attempting to hide just how painful it was. Severe leg cramping did not fit this romantic moment.

"It's okay," I gasped. "My legs are just a little tired. I probably just need to stretch out a little."

Steve did his best to help stretch my feet. Finally, unable to contain my pain any longer, I let out a strangled cry.

Steve looked at me, shocked, "What's wrong? Did I hurt you?" The cramps had spread to my calves, then my hamstrings and quads. It was excruciatingly painful.

I had no choice but to tell the truth. "My whole legs ..." I managed to get out as I tried to reach for my legs.

He understood and tried to massage them as best as he could. All I could do was point and nod. I had no choice but to be authentic. And right now, it was authentic agony. Here I was on our first date, trying to impress him. Instead, I had huffed and puffed my way up a mountain in too-tight jeans and, when we finally made it to the top, ended up writhing in pain on the ground wearing nothing but a wet t-shirt and underwear! Not quite the interlude I had imagined for myself.

THE HEART OPENS

When we first become involved in a relationship it exists in a state of rosy perfection. There are qualities that draw us to them, make us admire them, or feel we can open up to them. Perhaps we appreciate their keen insights into life, their sense of humor, or the fact they are self-made. Perhaps we like who we are when we are with them. They might make us feel we can be ourselves in their presence. Perhaps we are more easygoing, more organized, healthier, or just plain nicer. These are all wonderful things about ourselves that we experience in the presence of our loved one.

This unique coalescence of internal and external forces creates space for the heart to open and love naturally flows. We exist in a state of love where the mind takes a back seat to our open heart, and the obstacles of life don't touch us in the same way. We are so fully grounded in our heart-experience that we tend to stay out of the drama, the mental patterns of resistance and reactivity.

We experience a sense of wholeness, peace and contentment far beyond the confines of the thinking mind. Separation, within ourselves and with others, dissolves. This experience feels right. It feels as if the thing we have been missing and searching for our whole lives has arrived.

But there is one hitch. Because this expansive oneness seems only to happen in the presence of this person, we need them to continue to make us feel good. How do they do that? By being the person that caused us to open up to them in the first place.

And so, while the first experience of falling in love is spontaneous and effortless, we subtly try to secure this euphoria, trying to make it a constant state rather than a transient one. We unconsciously sense what the other wants and needs to maintain an openhearted stance to life. We take it upon ourselves to provide the other what they need to feel open, happy and in love. And, if we're in a relationship that "works," the other will do the same for us. We only show certain sides of our character, playing up what pleases our loved one. And we don't do it just for them; we do this for ourselves too. If they are our source, it is in our best interests to keep them in a state where they continue to shine love and affection on us. Essentially we stack the deck in our favor, to experience love, and avoid being deprived of it.

Often, we'll even do things we are not particularly interested in. We may see movies we secretly have no interest in, or profess our love of hiking all the while trying to hide the fact that we feel as if our heart is about to leap out of our chest and land on the trail in front of us while doing it. Perhaps we let our loved one think we love to cook when the last time we saw a kitchen was when our mother came to visit. Or, we may hide the fact we secretly like to eat in bed every now and then and prefer tabloids to literature.

But this is not a one-sided endeavor. The other person is doing the same for us as well. They go to "chick-flicks," wear shirts they normally wouldn't be caught dead in, stop seeing the friends we don't approve of, and very attentively listen to the same emotional dramas that will one day evoke a semi-comatose response.

In essence, we're both playing roles in a carefully constructed system of exchange, an unconscious game of "I'll be what you want, if you'll be what I want." That is not to say the other person does not have qualities we appreciate and love, but it does mean we tend to have a preference for those qualities that fit our ideal picture and make us feel good.

Throughout the week, Steve and I continued to get to know one another. I told him all about Daren and my heartbreak. I confessed Daren was the love of my life and if he ever asked me to be with him, I would not hesitate to say yes. Steve in turn told me about his previous relationships, and his current angst with the direction his life was going. We found unconditional receptivity in one another, which helped us come to peace within ourselves.

At the end of the week, Steve went back to the Netherlands. As luck would have it, my father and I were coming to the Netherlands the following week to lead a seminar. I would be teaching the yoga classes, and Steve and I planned to meet up. I even worked up the courage to tell my father about us. He was very calm and open. He understood that his little girl was going to be involved in a relationship at some point and he graciously let go.

CHAPTER SIX

MY RELATIONSHIP WITH STEVE developed from there. He came to the yoga center in the States for a three-month program called spiritual lifestyle training. He was not supposed to be actively involved in any relationships, so we did what anyone else in our situation would do, we snuck around.

We passed notes, and met surreptitiously after hours. "I will pick you up at the end of the driveway at 7pm," I wrote. "Wear a hat and scarf. If someone is around, I will drive by."

We'd go for dinner, scanning the parking lot for cars we recognized. We would meet in empty offices my friends on staff obligingly made available for us. Apparently, our little trysts were common knowledge, but the staff wanted to help us have our fun without letting on.

Steve knew I was inexperienced, and out of respect said he wanted to take things very slowly. He enjoyed the uncomplicated purity of our relationship, and though I had no interest in slow, was touched by his gentlemanly approach. I found it wonderfully old-world, and conceded to his wishes.

After nine months of "taking it slow," I'd had enough. I bought condoms myself and said it was time. We made love. Steve was my first. We were truly in love. We talked to each other on the phone nearly every day when we were apart. Traveling back and forth to the Netherlands to lead workshops, I would stay on to have time with him.

The following year, I moved to Holland and we began living together. I had moved for Steve, but was also looking for my own identity, separate from my father, the Guru, and the yoga center. Though the limitations of my teenage years had lifted, I felt I needed to find myself independent of my role as "the daughter of...". But the life I wanted was still a reaction to the one I'd had. I wanted freedom. I didn't want to be controlled or told what to do. Three thousand miles and another continent would do the trick, I thought. In truth, I might have left my past behind physically, but it was still with me and eventually I'd have to face it.

TRAINING EACH OTHER

Steve and I each brought our individual expectations to the relationship. I expected to be kissed, held, and generally treated as the central theme of his existence. His expectations of me were: She should listen to me, let me be as I am, give me space when I want it, and not try to boss me around or tell me how I should be doing things differently.

At the outset, we were both willing to accommodate the other's expectations. I didn't question his choices. He would cuddle with me as much as I wanted. But we still subtly trained one another to meet our desires. Steve felt the weight of my displeasure when he forgot my birthday. I felt his thunderous silence when I tried to make "suggestions" about his career. Conversely, when he did something like pick me up at the airport bearing flowers, my pleasure was unmistakable. When I gave him space to be alone or with his friends, his open demeanor showed me how much he appreciated the time without the complaints. Consciously we were "letting each other know" what worked for us. But we were also unconsciously "training" each other in our likes and dislikes. Not right or wrong, but definitely how it worked.

I like to call this training the "carrot and the stick" method. When our partner does what we want they get the "carrot." When they do something displeasing, it's the "stick." We all have varying methods by which we wield the carrot and the stick, but wield them we do.

That is how I "taught" Steve to be the sensitive man I wanted. Whenever I was upset about something, I would withdraw all my loving energy. I would only respond monosyllabically to anything he said unless he asked, "What's going on?"

Only then would I respond. If he tried to talk me out of what I was feeling, I would shut down–dead end. If he tried to defend himself it would end in a fight. Wrong way! Turn around and go back to where you started! If he just listened, I would soften and sometimes cry. If he tried to stop me from crying, I would get quarrelsome. But if he just let me have my feelings, listened and held me–Bingo! If he held me and stroked my head–even better. It would all be over fairly quickly and painlessly. That was the carrot. Then, after all that, if he had something to say back to me, I was able to listen openly and non-defensively–carrot with a cherry on top.

CONTROL

Soon, we began alternating between trying please each other and trying to *change* each other. In one sense, it was a process of vying for control. Who would get to set the standard of how the other should be? And who would be the one to comply with the standard? This was part of establishing a sort of pattern in the relationship that, once set, was unlikely to change. I would try to persuade Steve to get the kind of job I thought he should have. I tried to see how far I could push him before he would push back. He would try to tell me how I should cook Indian food–I *am* Indian. He was testing the borders of how far I would go to please him.

The degree to which we can get the other person to fit our picture is directly proportionate to the degree of control one person or the other has in the relationship. This is important because the more control one person has in the relationship, the more they can rely on securing happiness through it.

Happily, Steve and I established a fairly balanced division of authority, so that neither of us felt unduly controlled by the other. This was due to the fact we were pretty equally matched in stubbornness. It also didn't hurt that, having honed our communications skills; we were able to interact skillfully.

Since then, however, I have been in relationships where this was not the case. I have been so reliant on my partner for my happiness that I completely gave up who I was to fit what my partner wanted. I did this to get the love I thought I needed. But in doing so, I also gave up all control or authority in the relationship and put myself in a very precarious position. For anyone who has been there, it is not hard to see how this dynamic can quickly become abusive. The abuser is the one who has the control–who has successfully gotten the other person to give up who they are entirely to fit what the abuser wants. The one who is abused accepts this role to secure the love he or she so desperately wants. It is a symbiotic relationship, with each person playing their role and each person using either control or being controlled as a means to an end–love.

PERPETUATING THE ILLUSION

In many ways we construct a "perfect partner" in the play of our lives. And we have determined what that character does, says, and likes, long before a real person arrives to fill the role. This creates an initial relationship dynamic where we are blind to who the other person really is. It may be in part because they show only what they know we will like. It's also likely we don't *want* to see who the other person truly is; focusing instead on the character we've created. We see the other through the rose colored glasses of our inner fantasy. While one part of us may register the truth, another part doesn't want to see it…so we don't.

We put our partner in a proverbial box as if to say, "This is who you are. This is how you are supposed to act." But at some point, who they really are, will begin to stick out. Stray arms and legs begin to pop out of the box here and there. Now we have two options:

1. Denial: Turn a blind eye to all the parts sticking out, and pretend that they do in fact "fit."

2. Control: Try to train and coax, manipulate or pressure them back into the box. We try to get them to stop being who they are so they fit the picture we want.

I began with a cocktail of both strategies in varying measures at different times. Since we've already discussed the dynamic of control, let's explore denial.

DENIAL

In the beginning, I thought it was very romantic Steve wanted to "wait." He was a gentleman. My inexperience and not wanting to face facts let me ignore the obvious truths. I never questioned that a 26-year-old heterosexual male wanted to wait a year or even longer to have sex. Whenever I had initiated it, he said he wanted to preserve his "spiritual energy." He'd had sexual relationships with so many women; he wanted something different with me. I was special, and pure. And he wanted more than sex. Brought up in the tradition of yoga, and not wanting to look too closely, I accepted his explanation.

At the same time, I had many romantic pictures about what a relationship looked like. In my picture, the man would find me not only irresistibly beautiful, but also sensual and sexy. He would want to have sex with me all the time.

There were many other parts of my picture, though, that were met and exceeded. Steve was loving in a way I had never before experienced. He accepted me exactly as I was, my thoughts, my moods and my reactions. He would actually listen to all the minute details of my life, and I to his. He was attentive, having meals ready when I came home, and often massaging my back in the middle of the night when it would chronically ache. He could also be grouchy, moody and bossy. But that I had the capacity to allow for. It was not one of the lynch pins that made up my idea of a romantic relationship. In truth, he was a remarkable human being. Yet this one thing, first just beginning as a whisper, began to grow.

When I would initiate any kind of physical contact with a sexual undertone, Steve would withdraw. He felt uncomfortable. In the beginning, I didn't take much notice. I thought it was just a passing mood. I told myself, "Well, he just doesn't feel like it now, but later he will." We were intimate about once every two weeks, if I was lucky.

But in my picture, it "should" have been more often. And because reality didn't measure up to my picture, I began to feel that something was lacking. Romance novels had given me detailed information on how many times "other people" have sex per week. When this quota was not matched, our sex life started to look like a problem. Had I not been attached to this idea, I would not have been upset about it. There are many people who don't have an ideal of frequent sex in a relationship and therefore don't have a problem going long periods of time without it. Steve was one of those people. I was not.

Bottom line: I wasn't getting what I needed. But whether that need was real or based on comparison to an ideal was unclear. Looking back, it was likely both. I did have unrealistic romance-novel ideas about sex, but I also had a very real need for a certain amount of ongoing sexual chemistry, which was not happening.

To continue seeing the relationship as something I dearly wanted, I chose to suppress not only the reality of who Steve was, but also the reality of what I needed. I was determined to hold on to the idea that I had found my perfect mate and nothing, not even reality, was going to mess with that.

THE FANTASY CANNOT WITHSTAND REALITY

Reality, no matter how much we try to ignore it, has a nasty habit of intervening. As it becomes more and more clear that our partner is unable to maintain the fairytale we expect, we choose from our arsenal of denial (insisting on our fantasy) or control (finding a way to get them to be who we want). Eventually, no amount of control, coaxing or training is enough to get them to go back into the box we created for them. And no amount of denial can cover up the fact that this person is a very different one from the one we thought we got into relationship with. When neither denial nor control work, we get mad. It's called blame.

"Where is the person who hung on my every word? Every detail of my daily dramas?" we ask. "Where is the guy who used to wear those nice shirts?" He went the same way we did when we finally confessed our utter lack of interest in hiking, started schlepping around the house in oversized t-shirts, and even started pulling out the tabloids in favor of the epic novel we've been pretending to read for two years.

For the most part, we accept these truths in each other as they show themselves. The more we let go of our fantasy, the more we see and are seen for who we really are. We don't have to spend as much effort to impress because we can relax and know we are loved as we are.

But we all have elements of the fairytale partner we are attached to. The ones we depend on to make us feel good. Often, it is why we got into the relationship in the first place. When these begin to fall away, we don't let them go easily. This is what we are counting on to make us happy. When it appears we are not going to get what we wanted, we try to hold on. When that doesn't work, we get angry and we blame them for it.

We might say, "You didn't show me who you really are." And we'd be right. But is it not also equally true we didn't show all of who we are to them? Wasn't this a mutually agreed upon game? Most of us do not recognize this, however. And in the end, we may end up feeling betrayed, when in fact it was our expectation that was betrayed.

This is one of life's ultimate ironies. We make-up who the other person should be and they do their best to fulfill it. When they can't, we get mad at *them*. But the odds were stacked against them. How can we expect anyone to be different than they are? How can we expect them to play a false role for the rest of their lives, denying who they are, just so we can be happy? We know how it feels when the shoe is on the other foot. When someone expects us to be different than who we are. We know how hard we try to please them. But at some point a choice has to be made; either we are taken as we are, or we give up who we are in favor of how the other wants us to be. And I for one know how terrible the latter choice feels. I would not wish that on anyone, yet it is exactly what we implicitly ask each other to do in a partnership.

CHAPTER SEVEN

THOUGH ALL THE SIGNS were there that Steve would not live up to my idea of who he should be, I chose not to see it. But as time passed, and the box began to fall away, I had no choice but to see the reality of what was there. Steve did not want to have sex as much as I did. Period. That was a fact. Yet the more I tried to get him to fit into the mold I had created, the more obvious it became he could never hope to fit it. So I blamed him for not trying. When he did try, he was unhappy because he couldn't be himself. He had to choose. He could suppress who he was for years to come in order to keep me happy, or he could break out of the box I had put him in and be who he was. He broke out.

The more obvious the truth became, the less I wanted to see it. I first saw it with shocking clarity just before our wedding. A well-to-do friend offered us a romantic evening alone in her New England mansion. We had wine, baked Brie and crackers, with plush robes and towels for the Jacuzzi. The lights were dimmed, quiet music played in the background and we made our way to the deck. The night sky was filled with brightly shining stars. We held hands in awe, enjoying the simple pleasure of each other's company under nature's canopy.

With deep sighs of release, we lowered ourselves into the steaming water. The conversation was easy and open, interspersed with playful kisses and cuddles.

As we emerged from the hot tub, we showered poolside, toweled off and donned our robes.

"I have a surprise for you," I said. "Wait here and then come upstairs when I call you."

Earlier that day I had gone out to purchase a beautiful nightgown. It was elegant yet sexy. That was how I liked to think of myself. I wanted this time to be memorable and special. And for me that included an evening of leisurely lovemaking.

Excited, I hastily lit the candles in our bedroom, fluffed my hair and applied some lip gloss. I put massage lotion I had brought in my handbag on the bedside table. Massages are always a good place to start, I thought.

I arranged myself carefully on the bed and called out, "I'm ready. You can come up now."

I heard Steve's footsteps coming up the stairs. This was the first time I had ever done anything so forward. I had read this was what men liked, and I was certain Steve would find it as exciting as I did.

His outline shadowed the door. "What are you doing? What is all this?" he asked, genuinely taken aback.

"I wanted to have a special evening for us tonight." Code for, "Let's make love."

He stepped into the room and flipped on the lights. His open and easy demeanor of just minutes before had changed.

"I'm tired," he said as he flopped on the bed, arms crossed over his body, shoulders tensed. "Can't we just go to bed?" Code for, "I feel pressured, and I don't want to."

Until this time, I had always managed to tell myself things would change. Steve had told me he felt guilty about having sex with me. He was Catholic and I told myself that was why. I thought with time and my love that would change. He would see there was nothing to feel guilty about. This was the first time I actually saw it was very possible this would never change. Steve was how he was. Most likely he was not going to miraculously change into an amorous lover who could not get enough of me. In that moment of clarity, I knew this was what would eventually end our relationship. I believe many of us recognize the seed in the beginning that will eventually cause the end.

These insights all came in a fraction of a second. What came next was the question. Did I really want to get married knowing this was how it could be for the rest of our lives?

Instead of having sex that night, I told Steve I wasn't sure that I wanted to marry him. I didn't know if I could live with it. He listened impassively. What could he say or do? He couldn't force himself to have sex with me. To add to it, the more I wanted to have sex, the more he felt pressured. He felt he had to be something else than what he was to be loved. That "something else" was my idea of how he should be in that moment. The more I tried to fit him into a box, the less accepted he felt and the less he could relax enough to let his sexuality show itself.

We stayed up late into the night having made a pact we would never go to sleep with bad feelings between us. I told him about my fears for a future where my desire to experience passion wasn't met. He had been, after all, my only lover. He pointed out we did have sex–just not with the frequency I wanted. And when we did, I enjoyed it. He was right. Though we hadn't come to any final conclusions, our hearts were open and we fell asleep in each other's arms.

The next morning, I woke up to find this letter on my pillow.

I feel so good to be with you. All the things I say about myself, positive and negative, I feel you accept. Every time I tell you more, I see myself, how I am and how I have been. That helps me accept myself and not judge myself so harshly. I trust you and you make me trust myself. With that trust I dare to grow more. I dare to face things. I dare to face other people. You support me in that process.

But sometimes I don't feel secure and doubt if you will really keep supporting me. If you really do take me as I am. Knowing that, I try to be whatever I think you want me to be–happy, spontaneous, sympathetic, virile, and sexy. Anything but me.

I know I will always have doubts, not only about you, but also about anyone, anything, as long as I don't trust myself and accept myself. When I can accept myself as I am, I won't need to depend on you to accept me.

When I don't need you to accept me I can love you exactly as you are. I can love you whether you accept me or not--whether you marry me or not because, regardless, you have been an important part of my life.

The love that flows through me I direct to you out of gratitude that you are just you. And you are a most beautiful person who, in this very moment as I write this, I love unconditionally.

With peace in mind
And love in heart, Steve

This letter would turn out to encapsulate much of what we both knew intellectually, but had to learn experientially over the course of our relationship. We each have a set of unspoken conditions that when met, keep us in a loving interaction with life and our loved ones. When those conditions are met, when traffic goes our way, when the lines aren't long, when we get a raise or receive the recognition we think we deserve, and when we have the kind of physical intimacy we want, our conditions are met and we feel open, happy–loving to life. But in all of these cases, we are dependent upon circumstances to keep us happy. This is called conditional happiness. In a relationship, it is called conditional love. We are looking to the other to fill our pre-conditions to maintain a sense of well-being.

But we can also use the relationship to practice letting go of the need for the other to be different than they are. When we don't need them to be different, we love them as they are. Then love is present whether our preferences are met or not. Our love stands apart from what they do or don't do, say or don't say.

Knowing this was no replacement for experience. The seed of us that was planted put us both through a growth process that would teach us to love beyond our expectations. But the only way to get there was to begin with the hopes, dreams, and expectations we did have, and allow them to be dismantled one by one.

Steve's letter struck the center of my heart. This was a very special human being with whom I had been gifted. I had done nothing I knew of to deserve him. His presence in my life felt like the greatest gift God had ever given me. And I knew the openness we shared was rare by any standards. Was I willing to give all that up because I didn't feel sexually acknowledged by Steve in the way I thought I should be? After all, how many hours in a day would we be having sex? Statistically, it was small compared to the time we would spend interacting in so many other ways, and these other ways worked. I made my choice. I knew when I looked at other relationships, this was the one I wanted, and Steve was the person I wanted. Any doubts stemming from my own needs were brushed aside. My overwhelming feelings for Steve, and the value of the relationship we could so clearly have, triumphed. My faith was restored that if we loved each other enough, things would change.

Two years after we had met and lived together, Steve and I married. The issue of sex was ever-present between us, but it seemed to come and go. We could talk it out, and that helped me move through my own resistance. Through it all, the love between us was undeniable.

Steve's entire family and many close friends had come from Holland to the United States to celebrate our wedding. The 200 plus guests gathered at a Vanderbilt Estate in the Berkshire Mountains. The poolside ceremony was held under large Moroccan-style canopied tents decorated with satins in tones of burgundy and gold.

We went on a honeymoon to Maine. I had many ideas about what our honeymoon would look like. Of course I had learned all about it from movies, television, magazines and romance novels, and it was nothing like those. We boated, swam, did yoga, cooked, played Scrabble and explored the surrounding towns.

When I was able let go of the idea it was supposed to be different, I was happy. My fulfillment came from being completely present with Steve and the experiences we were having, just as they were. The simple act of having tea on the deck cuddled together in blankets as we watched the sunrise was magical. As we came up with obscure and sometimes outlandish words to use all of our Scrabble squares, I felt deeply content. But as my mind went to what might come after an evening game, I was divided. I could no longer enjoy the game and be fully satisfied by it. My mind was preoccupied with the next thing. Would he feel like having sex tonight? Should I put on my sexy nightgown? Would that be pressuring him? What if he didn't feel like it? All of these conflicting thoughts took me out of the contentment and peace I found in just being with the experiences just as they were.

Relaxing With What Is

As my dad would say, "Nothing is a problem until you decide there's a problem." As long as I didn't decide things should be different than they were, there was no problem. I could experience contentment with more and more things even though they might not have been my first preference.

If we are sitting at a red light we have the choice to experience that red light in one of two ways—we can resist it or allow it. If we resist we suffer, because the act of wishing it to be different causes conflict with the way it is. It is the conflict we experience as stress, not the red light itself.

If, on the other hand, we can simply allow for the fact the light is red and relax with how it is, it ceases to assault us in the same way. We might have a preference for the light to be green, but we can accept and relax with how it is. By changing how we are with circumstances, we change our experience of them. The formula is this: external events combined with internal reactions create the final outcome. It is not just how my partner is that determines my happiness, but how I internally *choose to be* with those external circumstances that determine the final outcome.

In marriage, Steve offered me many "red lights." And I offered many to him. If I could relax with his quirks and let them be, they weren't a problem. But the moment I decided he should be less bossy or more communicative, I suffered. Like the red light, he could not be any different than he was in any given moment. It was already happening. He could be different in the *next* moment, but not in this one. Depending on how I chose to be with that slice of reality, I could suffer, or I could create a measure of peace. The choice was mine.

With a commitment to practice, we can let go of more than we hold on to and in so doing build a relationship where love is experienced more, and resistance less.

In a way, this is a backdoor to the love and fulfillment most of us so desperately want. We can find fulfillment by changing how we are with any circumstance. Of course, this will not happen with all things all of the time, nor should it. But the more we develop our ability to allow our loved one and ourselves to be as we are, the more we naturally experience the one thing we desire most: love.

CHAPTER EIGHT

NOT LONG AFTER our wedding, Steve and I were in the shop at my father's yoga center. I was looking at clothes and he was rifling around the music section. Without really knowing why, I glanced up. To my shock, not 20 feet away from me was Daren! I could not believe it. I had not seen him for years, but had heard about what he was up to "through the grapevine." He had, through an unforeseeable series of events, become hooked into the Hollywood crowd. He had worked as a personal yoga trainer and guide on many movie sets, with all kinds of A-list stars from Demi Moore to Woody Harrelson. I have never hyperventilated before or since, but the shock of seeing him sent me spinning, and I could not control it.

Steve turned to me, "What is wrong with you? Why are you breathing like that?"

With one hand on my mouth trying to control my breath, I raised the other towards Daren. "That's him," I said. "That's Daren."

Steve is not the jealous type, and in the entire life of our relationship this was the only time I ever saw it. He could plainly see my visceral reaction and remembered one of our first conversations when I told him Daren was the love of my life.

Daren had not seen us yet. Steve threw an assessing glance over his shoulder and then authoritatively took my hand.

"Let's go," he said. "Let's get out of here." Still breathing shallowly, but more composed, I took his hand and began to follow him out of the store.

Just as we were passing, Daren looked up. Our eyes caught and held. Recognition dawned.

"Kamini!" he said in that same resonant voice that had always turned my insides to jelly. "It is so good to see you. I was hoping I'd run into you!" he exclaimed.

He was clearly delighted to see me, and I was happy to see him. But there was one thing he didn't know, and that one thing would change everything.

"I want to introduce you to someone," he said, gesturing to his right. I had been so occupied with Daren I hadn't noticed who was standing next to him. Woody Harrelson. At any other time, Woody would have likely been the focus of my attention. I would have been tickled to meet such a well-known personality. But at this moment, all my focus was on Daren–and Steve. This situation was feeling stickier by the minute.

I turned to Woody, shook hands and made all the customary remarks.

Then I turned to introduce Steve. "This is Steve," I said, pausing briefly. "My husband."

I put just enough emphasis on that second sentence to get my point across. I could not be with him the way we used to be. I couldn't even really talk. Steve was at, and over, his edge. I could feel it. And my loyalty was to him now, not to my past. No matter how compelling it was.

I could see Daren's face change. He had not known. No one had told him. Years later I would learn he had come back in part to see if the time was right for us to be together. But clearly that was not the case. He had to let go right then and there. Our dream of us was over.

"Are you coming to the dance class?" he said, recovering his composure. "You both need to come. Please come," he said. His gazed fixed on mine. He was trying to tell me something with his eyes. It was his way of creating closure.

"Okay," I replied. "We have to change, but we'll be there shortly."

As we walked out, Steve said, "You're not really going to class are you? You are not well. You're still not breathing okay."

"I need to do this Steve," I replied. "We can't just not show up after I said we'd be there. Come with me."

Reluctantly, Steve assented. We dressed and made our way in stilted silence to the class. That class was my farewell to Daren, ironically at the place where we had once so deeply connected. At different points, his eyes would connect with mine–communicating his hopes for us, regret, and finally completion. Not a word was spoken. Like so many times before, circumstances kept us from talking. This was the end of our story. For now…

DEVELOPING THE CAPACITY TO RELAX WITH WHAT IS

Relationships can be about expanding our capacity to experience love, fulfillment and contentment with each other the way we are and relax into it. That said, there are things that put us in physical or psychological danger that are never advisable to relax with. Just get out.

Sometimes we may appear to accept the other person, but instead we are secretly keeping an internal checklist of everything we have "forgiven" the other person for. It may appear we have accepted, but in fact, have only suppressed our resentment. The next time a fight erupts we will surely pull out the list of all our "rights" and our partner's "wrongs." Hidden resistances wait in storage until they finally find an outlet. And when they do, they all come pouring out–even years later. Many of us end up doing this, thinking we are authentically practicing unconditional love. It is not the same thing. The way to know is if we are experiencing greater peace or greater resentment as a result of what we are doing.

What we are capable of relaxing with exists on a continuum. There are the easy things, like the toilet seat, the toothpaste cap and the dishes. There are the personality quirks like the tendency to interrupt, forget appointments, drive over the speed limit or not take things as seriously as we might.

Then there are the core issues in the relationship, which often center around things like money, sex, decision-making power, division of labor, or confronting the past. These core issues are the most challenging. Usually they are the issues we interpret to mean something about us as a person. Because it feels personal, it is more likely to trigger our gut-level defenses. For me, the sexual issue struck closer to the center of my relationship with Steve. For him, it was my past with Daren.

While incidental irritations will, for the most part, dissolve away or diminish with practice, the trajectory is often less clear-cut as issues hit closer to home.

We might find we can relax with a particular issue some of the time. We might even think it has gone the way of lesser irritations. But before we know it, we find ourselves back to being triggered all over again. This is not a failure. It is natural. It is natural to feel jealous, insecure, angry, and anything else we might happen to be feeling. But each time we do succeed, we are teaching ourselves to move in a life direction that is, on the whole, filled with greater peace.

Like lifting weights, it is advisable to start with "lighter weights," or more incidental irritations, before working up to the heavier ones requiring more strength, skill and self-awareness. If we're paying attention, life organically teaches us how to do this. The things that once irritated us in young relationships simply roll off our backs now. We can see them with greater perspective. We know we've gone down the same road countless times before to no avail, and they just don't seem worth getting upset about anymore.

The truth is, there will always be some things we cannot relax with at all–nor should we expect to. The question is, can we relax with the fact that no matter what, there are some things we will just not be able to, or want to accept? If we fight with our lack of acceptance, we induce inner conflict. One part of us tries to wrestle the other part into trying to feel a certain way. It doesn't work. Now, instead of trying to put our partner in a box of how they should be, we put ourselves in one. The result is the same. Instead of being unable to love who the other is, we cannot accept who we are. If we can truly relax with the fact that we are angry, disappointed or frustrated, it can be allowed to exist without fighting it. It is not something we try to get rid of. Rather, we co-exist with it in a more easeful, less conflicted manner.

When we can't accept and instead react, we need to allow for the reaction, but not dismiss it. Take stock of what happened. Notice what the trigger was. Notice what was done and said and the effect it created. Watch and learn from what happened rather than indulging in self-justification or self-flagellation. We might ask ourselves how to do things differently next time so our words and deeds will move us towards harmony with ourselves and with the other. By noticing the connection between how we are and the results we are creating, we create an ideal environment for a natural course-correction. We all want positive results. If we can clearly see that what we are doing does not work, we will automatically begin to change our strategy without inducing inner conflict.

A DEEP AND ABIDING LOVE

The stages of relationships can organically lead to a deep and abiding love. My parents are one example. Ideal images gave way to reality. Reality gave way to control, blame, and eventually, acceptance. This is the opportunity relationships have always been offering us. But for most of us that possibility is obscured by the discomfort of the journey. The journey feels hard, uncomfortable and confrontational, so we assume something is wrong. But this is simply the process many relationships will go through. If we see this process as a problem, we will experience it as one. If we see it as an opportunity to create an experience of love and fulfillment independent of our flaws, or our partner's, that is what it can become.

We cannot get where we want to go unless we are willing to begin where we are. Like a loaf of bread, we can't get to the slice we want until we go through all the ones before it (and in life we can't cheat by jumping ahead). If we can bring this process to conscious awareness, we can speed it up, and maybe avoid the pitfalls. And if we can't avoid them, we can at least understand what is happening.

As we use relationships as a place to deeply relax with the way things are, we find peace with who the other is and who we are. The fights, disagreements, and irritations are experienced as waves on the surface of the ocean. They are what comes and goes. But love becomes the constant like the deep, quiet depths of the ocean. It is not called into question every time one partner or the other is unhappy. It is the ever-present background in front of which our ever-changing moods, feelings and dramas play out.

Doesn't This Practice Make Me a Pushover?

Moving towards this kind of relationship does not mean we are spiritual pushovers. We need to recognize what our boundaries are and communicate them clearly. Not as threats, but as information. As a parent, we may not have control over how our children ultimately behave, but that does not mean there will be no *consequences* for those behaviors. Just because there are consequences for a child's behavior doesn't mean we don't love them.

We will make choices and take certain actions in response to the choices and actions our partner makes. The test will be to notice if the steps we take in response to what the other does are vengeful, hurtful or retaliatory—or are they simply what we need to do for ourselves to maintain our own sense of integrity? Ideally, the action we are taking is simply the outcome of the behavior that created it. It's an appropriate response to actions that do not work within the context and responsibilities of the relationship.

Will and Surrender Are the Keys to Empowerment in Relationship

The practice of expanding our capacity to love has a willful component and a surrendered component. We begin by allowing for the fact things are the way they are. We don't try to deny it, or get upset about it. The milk is already spilled. From there we take willful steps, like communication, making requests, and making changes. We do everything we can to move ourselves in the direction we need to go. We are not passive victims of life. But when we have done everything we can, it is time to let go; surrender to the way things are right now (because, in fact, they cannot be any different in that moment). But it doesn't necessarily end there. We may again survey the current status of a situation. We may re-assess and from a relaxed and open stance to what is, initiate a next set of actions and words that again move us in a direction that feels right. This continual dance between will and surrender is a key to letting go of our conditions of the other while allowing ourselves to be fully self-expressed and empowered beings.

In one of the ancient texts of India called the Bhagavad Gita, Lord Krishna says, "you have the right to action, not the results of action." We take the steps we need to take and say what we need to say. It is our responsibility to fully express (with skill) our feelings, wants and needs. That is our way of acknowledging who we are as we are right now. But we cannot make the other do what we want. That is beyond our control.

Releasing attachment to a certain outcome will often yield a more open and positive response than we ever hoped for. But things won't always go our way. Whatever the result, desirable or undesirable, we have gained information. That information can serve as an important guidepost to help ascertain our next steps.

Before I could accept Steve, I blamed him. If only Steve would change this one little thing. I tried to reason him into wanting sex more often. I tried to find out what I was doing wrong. I did everything I could think of to get him to do what I wanted. I blamed him for being stubborn. How hard could it be? Did he not love me enough to try? Isn't it just one of those things that you put your mind to and make it work?

After the blame came truth. How I felt. What I really needed and wanted from him as my husband. After much discussion, I was able to formulate some clear requests without any subtext of guilt or resentment to get him to do what I wanted.

Finally, Steve agreed to some therapy sessions. I made a clear set of requests, but he fulfilled them in a way that was workable and congruent with who he was. The outcome, however, was not what I had hoped for.

The advice from Steve's therapist was clear and simple. I should take a step back, stop making demands and take pressure off him. I complied. While this was excellent advice, it did not have *my* desired effect. Without my voicing my wants and needs on a regular basis, our sex life dwindled to almost nil. A number of other attempts also sputtered to a halt. The reality was clear. I had done what I could, said what I needed to say, and Steve had done his part to the degree he was able. Nothing had changed. I had taken action, which I had the right to, but I also had to surrender to the results. That was outside my circle of influence.

Of course that didn't mean I had to surrender for good. I just needed to relax with the outcome of this particular episode. I then had to take that outcome and the information that came as a result and take the next step that felt right.

Many of us who embark on this practice miss this point. In the name of accepting the other as they are, we often deny ourselves. We suppress who we are, our thoughts, feelings, desires, and reactions and call it being unconditional. But true unconditional love means not only letting the other person be who they are, it also means letting ourselves be as we are. When we miss this key, a relationship in which we seem to be letting go can actually become a medium through which we close down our self-expression, and with it our life energy.

As insignificant as my need to be sexually met in the relationship may seem to some, it was real for me. And in the name of accepting Steve unconditionally, I subtly began to deny myself.

CHAPTER NINE

O UT OF THE IDEAS other people, books, and society had given me, I created a picture of an ideal relationship out of thin air. When Steve did not meet that manufactured picture, I first thought something was wrong with him. Then I decided something was wrong with me. It never occurred to me nothing was wrong with either of us. It was comparison to a pre-conceived notion that made us both appear insufficient and imperfect. But I did not recognize this. Instead, Steve appeared lacking in reference to my idea of how he should be. And if Steve wasn't the problem, then I must be the one who was lacking. After all, the picture was the one solid truth that was unchangeable—wasn't it? This was how things were *supposed* to be. Everybody knew that. And if the picture wasn't coming to fruition because of Steve, there was only one other factor that could be the cause—me.

It never occurred to me to question the one thing that was causing all this suffering in the first place—the supposed truth of my picture. Who said that love has to take one particular form and look one particular way? Doesn't it come in many forms? As many forms as there are people? Who is to say one form is better than the others? Well, for one, I did. I believed it hook, line and sinker. And I suffered for it.

If Steve wasn't the problem and I was, what was wrong with me? All I had to do was look to the gap between me, and my ideal image. It told me what I had to fix about myself. And, as that ideal promised, if I could just fix those things I would be lovable. Then Steve would love me in the way that I wanted. He would find me sexy and beautiful, and I would be happy.

The gap between who I was and who I thought I should be was obvious. In comparison to what I believed I should be, I had too many curves. I didn't have porn star boobs and a flat stomach. I was too much of a friend and not enough of a sex kitten. I was not beautiful enough. My hair was too long. I didn't wear the right clothes. I was too weak to stand up for myself. Yet I judged myself for being too demanding by asking for what I wanted.

It was a dizzying list of contradictory inner-demands that I could not possibly fulfill. Enter inner-conflict. On the one hand I did my best; I starved myself. I tried to wear the right clothes, do my hair just right, and be the person I thought Steve would love. On the other hand, part of me was doing just the reverse. I ate more, exercised less. The more I tried to make myself be one way, the more another part of me did the complete opposite. Neither was me, and both felt terrible.

I began to lose my connection to my own essence. Everything I did felt wrong. Instead of being confident in myself and my way of being in life, I doubted every aspect of my being. I doubted the very things that made me beautiful and powerful and wonderful in my own right. The more I lost my connection to my essence, the more dependent I became on Steve to give me any sense of self worth I did have.

I became more possessive. My growing insecurity was equally matched by jealousy. I was afraid someone would take Steve away from me. I had very little access to myself as the source of my own happiness because I had doubted it away. I had compromised myself. Steve was all I had left.

LOSS OF SELF

I've seen this phenomenon set out in different ways in movies, books, and the lives of my friends. The details may not be the same, but the basic story is. Man falls in love with woman for who she is. Woman somehow feels she has to be different–she is not good enough as she is. So she goes about trying to change herself to fit some manufactured ideal of who she should be in relationship. In the process, she becomes a shadow of herself. She becomes totally dependent on the reactions of the man to give her a sense of self-worth because she has given away her own. But she has lost everything that was strong and beautiful about her that attracted the man to her in the first place. He is less attracted to her and begins to pull away. The more he pulls away, the more dependent and dis-empowered she becomes.

This does not happen because he did anything wrong or she did anything wrong. But because she believed in some picture of who she should be over the beauty of who she was. She gave herself away to some made up idea.

In my instance, Steve did not pull away. He was steady. But I did give up myself in favor of a picture of who I should be. I struggled with who I was. I even hated myself at times, convinced if only my body was different Steve would find me sexy.

If I could just have the perfect body, Steve would love me in the way I wanted him to love me. Of course, the irony in all of this is Steve did love me. With all his heart. He just loved me differently than what my picture allowed for. It never occurred to me that it was my stubborn allegiance to my picture of how I should be that caused me to hate myself, and blinded me to Steve's very real and enduring love for me. Instead, I believed I was at fault. If only I could be different I told myself, this wouldn't be a problem.

I don't believe Steve caused this insecurity. The situation triggered what I already, secretly thought about myself. I remember a time when Steve and I first met. On one of our first dates, he motioned me to come over and sit on his lap. Before I even sat down I said to him, "Am I too heavy?" He laughed and said, "How do I know? You haven't sat on my lap yet."

In the same way, my self-worth and my body were in question before Steve or this relationship ever came along. In fact, it was the question I was always asking life in every situation in one form or the other. Am I okay? Am I likeable? Am I worthy? Pretty much everything I did, everything I said, everything I achieved and the recognition I got served one question, "Am I good enough?" The funny thing was, part of me was looking for situations and people to validate me, yet when they did, I dismissed it.

I was coming to life with an assumption I was not worthy and then set about systematically negating any positive validation. If someone said, "Your teaching has come a long way," I translated it to, "Your teaching was really bad before." I craved feeling loved and accepted, yet I was unable to receive it. I would block my ability to receive encouragement by searching for, *or even making up*, subtle criticism.

This little habit was the one way I succeeded in driving Steve crazy. No matter what he said, I could twist it around. No matter how much he tried to make me feel better about myself or reassure me, I could turn a compliment into an insult. He said, "Your hair looks nice, you should wear it down more often." I heard, "I don't like it when you wear your hair up." He could say while we were in an intimate moment, "You are beautiful." But inside I would dismiss it as the heat of the moment. He was no match against my inner conviction that I did not measure up.

In this way, I caused much of my own suffering. I would pick apart every sentence, every look he made, or didn't make, to convince myself I wasn't good enough. Tuning out his protestations, I would go into full-fledged self-flagellation mode, beating myself up with my own inadequacies.

Why did I do this? The reason most of us do, I think. To get myself to change. To get myself to fit that ideal picture. If I felt badly enough about where I was, maybe someday I'd be able to squeeze myself into that picture. Then I would love myself, I would feel whole and I would be okay—and Steve would love me in the way I wanted to be loved.

THE EXTERNAL REVEALS OUR INSECURITIES

My father used to say that no one can cause us as much pain as we cause ourselves. In my case, this was true in so many ways. Steve helped co-create a certain climate in our relationship. But I took it and made it about me and my own inadequacies. He did not do that. I did.

Initially, I pinned this on him saying, "You made me feel insecure." But in retrospect I see it was an easy out to blame him for what I felt about myself.

My life had been dedicated to searching out instances which validated my fear of not being good enough. When circumstances came together in such a way to show me my own negative self-talk, I blamed the person through whom that tendency was shown. I chose to ignore the glaring truth–I was the one who carried that belief all along. Steve did not create that belief in me; he simply revealed its presence.

My colleague, Eric Walrabenstein, uses a great metaphor which I like to apply to relationship. We all carry within us underground seeds which often exist outside of our awareness. Those seeds could be of insecurity, not feeling good enough, or feeling that we don't measure up. When external weather conditions change, and events come together in a particular way, the environment is such that those seeds, previously invisible, grow into weeds. They become visible.

For me, the weather condition was the lack of sexual attention. Within that environment, the once-dormant seed of insecurity came to life and grew into a weed. To the untrained eye, it could appear that the weather (Steve's way of being) was the cause of the weed of insecurity. But if we were to look closer, we would see that the external conditions simply offered the environment in which that seed of insecurity could suddenly rise to the surface from the unseen to the seen. He did not *cause* the insecurity, he simply provided the environment in which insecurity, already present in seed form, could be revealed.

Not realizing this, most of us set about blaming or changing the weather as the apparent cause. We say, "He made me feel that way." If instead we were to look deeper, we might recognize that the weather conditions can actually reveal the parts of us that have long been hidden underground and therefore out of our reach. Then what looks like a problem caused by the other becomes an opportunity to learn about ourselves.

And, it is not that these seeds are revealing themselves to punish us. They are simply issues which have not been completed and are seeking healing. If we only try to change the weather (the other) without addressing the seed, it will naturally reappear again and again until we are ready to face it.

The good news is we never have to go searching for what we have not resolved. It can all be revealed through our relationships with others and with life if we are willing to look. We don't have to go looking for it, it is showing itself to us in every moment of our lives.

Not realizing the source of self-doubt lay within me; my own issues of self worth were increasingly pulling me into a quagmire of inner conflict and self-loathing. Instead of exploring the underground seed of "not being good enough," I vacillated between blaming Steve for not being able to fulfill my image of a husband, and blaming myself for not being able to fulfill my own image of a desirable wife. Both seemed like the obvious external cures to the sense of insecurity I always seemed to feel now.

In fact, neither one could solve the problem permanently until I recognized the seed of self-doubt lived within me, and could never be silenced indefinitely by Steve's love, or in an image of a "perfect" me. These could mask the seed, but the only thing that would neutralize it was addressing the true source of my suffering.

CHAPTER TEN

I FOUGHT WITH MYSELF to get to the place where I could be relaxed with our life as it was. But the more I fought with myself to feel differently than I did, the worse it became. My only avenue was to find peace with not being at peace, to allow myself to be in difficulty and resistance to myself and to Steve. I had to let myself be honest about where I was and talk about it.

But there was one thing I did not want to be honest about, even with myself. Just as the reality of Steve was that he had less of a sex drive than I did, my unacknowledged reality was that a fully-expressed sex life was something I really needed and wanted. But instead of acknowledging my reality, I only continued to acknowledge his. I focused my attention solely on accepting him as he was, rather than accepting my own needs as well. Instead, I suppressed them.

I knew many people in relationships who have differing sexual drives. In some the man has a stronger sex drive than the woman, in some relationships it was the other way around. I thought, "Why can't we be like them?" The difference it seemed was the partner who did not have their needs met could surrender to it. They could allow for the reality of the situation and be happy despite it.

But what about me? Why couldn't I do that? I knew all the "right" teachings. I knew what I was supposed to do. I was supposed to accept it, relax with it, and be happy with the beautiful relationship I *did* have. And I succeeded–to a degree. But there was something else equally true. I had never really known what it was like to be in a passionate, fully-expressed sexual relationship. And I wanted to know what it was like. It was as simple as that.

I couldn't be like "other people," because I wasn't "other people." I was me. I came into this life with my own set of circumstances. I was my own person. And just because some people could relax with it didn't mean I could. But instead of acknowledging that truth, I denied it. When I couldn't make myself feel differently, I simply pretended I didn't feel it. Just as I chose to be blind to who Steve was, I chose to be blind to who I was.

THE HIDDEN DOORWAY TO EMPOWERMENT

Just as will and surrender apply when we ask for changes in the other, the same applies to us. We may deliberately and willfully practice relaxing with things as they are, but we also have to surrender to the reality of our inner world as well. Rather than willfully trying to force ourselves to be okay with things as they are, we move *towards* relaxing with things as they are. But if our needs are still alive and kicking, we surrender to the feelings and reactions that are present.

Normally, our solution is control, and the excessive use of will. Just as we try to control the other to get them to be what we want, we try to control ourselves so we can show up in life and in relationships the way we think we should. This self-control commonly shows up as suppression, denying who we are so we can look like the person we think we should be. Using both will and surrender allows us to heed our own needs and boundaries.

THE BIGGEST PITFALL

Our biggest pitfall is that we dis-empower ourselves in the name of unconditional love. We understand our job is to accept the reality of what is. But we fail to recognize we are also part of that reality. We think that to practice unconditional love we have to deny our needs or wants. This could not be more untrue. It is the entire picture of reality that needs to be allowed for. There is no such thing as practicing unconditional love and then excluding ourselves from that very same experience of unconditional love. That is essentially saying, "Everything in existence is allowed to be exactly as it is in its fullness–except me." How is that uncon-ditional? A very important piece has been left out of the equa-tion. It is conditional love masquerading as unconditional love.

When we allow everyone else to be who they are by sac-rificing ourselves, we create profound internal imbalance. We stifle who we are; we talk ourselves out of our own needs. Or we simply pretend they do not exist. In the name of doing "the right thing," we end up cutting off our own acknowledgement of ourselves and what we need.

When we do this, a relationship in which we seem to be let-ting go can actually become a medium through which we close down our life energy. In the name of being the person who does everything right, we internally divide ourselves. Though we may appear to be at ease with life, with our relationships, we are not. The external war becomes an internal war fought late at night, in moments when we let our guard down and allow ourselves to feel the pain of what we have done to ourselves through our own self-denial.

I believe this profound internal division creates deep-seated stressors on the body and mind, which can manifest through physical symptoms ranging from weight changes, to pain and even illness.

Why did I deny my needs? If I did not, it would call my en-tire relationship with Steve into question. If I was really honest about who I was and what I needed, it might put me in a posi-tion where I had to choose myself over my relationship with him. Though I had my issues, I was not ready to even acknowl-edge the possibility. I didn't want to go there. I couldn't. Steve was everything to me and I couldn't imagine who I would be without him. He was my source of fulfillment.

Rather than risk losing that fulfillment and having to find it inside myself, it was much easier and more convenient to ig-nore my own needs and wants. Though they came up with ever-increasing force, I would simply try to push through them and try to get back to the "good stuff" I had with him. I did not want to look too closely lest my fragile construction of externally-sourced love collapse.

The most obvious manifestation of this convoluted internal dynamic was weight gain. I used food to cover up my urge to be desired as a woman. If I didn't feel it, I wouldn't have to acknowledge it was there. The more weight I gained, the less I felt I deserved to be in a sexually fulfilling relationship. "See?" my inner critic would say. "You really didn't deserve this after all. You are fat and ugly now, so stop wishing for something that will never be." In a way, this served me. If I had the weight, I was taking myself out of the game. I took away my own possibility of being seen as a sexually desirable woman. If the possibility was gone, maybe I would stop wanting it. Twisted, I know.

My own sense of unworthiness grew with the weight. With it, my inner fight continued. Part of me trying to be thin and seen as a sensual woman, part of me trying to hold on to the weight to smother those same needs. These two conflicting factions played out within me, and my body paid the price.

CHAPTER ELEVEN

URING THIS TIME Steve and I had lived in Holland and
then had moved back to the U.S. He worked closely
with my dad and I worked at an affiliated leadership
center. Now the weight really came on. Not only did I feel op-
pressed by my inner needs, but I was not happy where I was,
either. I had taken the job in the States because it made sense,
not because it made me happy. But the realization came too late.
The transition had already been made and I felt I could not go
back.

Now, I was not only ignoring my needs in my marriage, but
also my environment. It felt like I was making myself stay where
I was by weighing myself down. I was reducing my energy level
enough that I had no will to go anywhere but where I was.

Steve and I would talk about this. He would remind me
that we could leave at any time. But my mind couldn't compre-
hend another option. I felt like we'd committed to staying and
we had to. I felt boxed in.

Once, while we were living near the center, Daren came.
As usual, no one had told me he would be there. He was leading
a workshop for the dance teachers when I ran into him. The externally imposed distance was ever-present, but the feelings were
still alive. What could either of us say? Nothing. During my free
time, I attended some of his sessions. His teaching and presence,
independent of my attraction, had always kindled my own spirit
and made me feel alive. This time was no different. The dance
helped me remember myself again.

During those sessions I could see he was involved with one
of the women there. I recognized the same eye contact, the same
subtle attentions given to her over the rest of us. I had once been
the recipient of those attentions. But no more.

Just months later, fate took a hand. My father had no choice but to resign from the yoga center he had spent his entire life creating. It was time for my entire family to leave behind our world and all the people who had once been like family to us. Most I would never see again. My father and mother went to live in Florida with a loyal friend, my brother to Pennsylvania to manage the now vacated site of the original yoga center my father had started 20 years before.

Steve and I went to Michigan, where I had fortuitously received a job offer as Director of Wellness at an executive retreat center. The job was everything I hoped for, but I had still not recovered from the atom bomb of my father's loss, my mother's pain, and a very public loss of face. Steve was unhappy in isolated and conservative Michigan. He became depressed. I was still in shell shock.

After less than a year we agreed I would leave my job on one condition; we would move back to Holland. That was where we spent the next six years. We slowly built up a coaching, yoga and massage practice together and helped develop a yoga studio in the style of my father's teaching. We began doing trainings for businesses with the help of Steve's sister, and my good friend, Marjan. Eventually, we started a company which offered stress management services to businesses. Both of our reputations grew. We were featured in magazine articles and radio interviews, including Cosmopolitan magazine. We had everything going for us. With time, we had created the life and structure we wanted.

THE EDGE

To me, commitment to a relationship is a form. It is not just a symbol of love. It is a place within which we choose to practice love. When we commit, what we are committing to is our willingness to face what is present in the relationship without running away from it. We are saying, "No matter how much I want to resist you, I promise to do my best to relax with things just as they are, and in so doing find the fulfillment possible for me right here and now." A relationship then becomes the form within which we learn to expand our capacity to love and experience fulfillment and contentment. In order for this to be effective, we need to practice at the edge.

The concept of the edge, and in fact many of the principles outlined so far, comes from the original, authentic teachings of yoga. I have applied them as they have shown up in my life. One of the things that make the practice of yoga powerful is practicing at the edge.

In a yoga class, the yoga poses are the form within which we practice, and there are many ways they can be used. A primary purpose is learning to stay relaxed and open amidst the mental and emotional stress that results from trying to achieve or measure up to the pose. We do not necessarily become more skilled at the poses, but more skilled at maintaining internal steadiness amidst the pressures the pose exerts. We are training ourselves to create a different relationship with a mind that is constantly comparing, competing, avoiding discomfort or trying to measure up to some manufactured ideal. We are essentially training ourselves to have a mind, rather than be run by it.

If used correctly, yoga poses can teach us how to disengage from a mind that gets us into the comparing game. Instead, we cultivate the capacity to be at ease with the pose just as it is showing up–perfect, imperfect, comfortable or uncomfortable.

This skill translates to life. By increasing our capacity to stay relaxed under greater and greater pressures, we learn to interact with life's challenges more effectively. As a result, we accumulate less stress and experience greater harmony with the experience of each moment, whether it is perfect, imperfect, comfortable or uncomfortable.

In relationships, we are put in a psychic pose. Like the physical pose, we are learning to stay relaxed and open, but now in the midst of daily situations that would normally cause us to react and close down our heart to the experience. If we can learn how to close down less to life, we can experience happiness with more aspects of it.

Whether practicing the physical or the psychic pose, the edge is the place where physical resistance and mental reaction tends to arise. With deliberate and applied use of the tools of yoga, we are just able to manage the resistance or reaction, and stay relaxed. If that is not possible, the edge has been surpassed.

WHEN THE PRACTICE BECOMES TOLERANCE

If we are over the edge, we will not be able to relax amidst the mental and physical experience. We will just be tolerating it. The tendency will be to shut down, go into an internally defensive mode and try to "survive" until the pose is over. This does not serve the practice because it is not allowing us the opportunity to learn to relax. The intensity of the pose has become so overwhelming that the ability to relax with what is happening is inaccessible. In today's culture, the thinking is "more is better." However, in yoga that is not necessarily so. More can actually serve us less.

The habit of practicing beyond the edge does not just show up on the yoga mat. It also shows up in life. Some take spiritual teachings to mean whatever our lot in life, it is spiritual to suffer through it. In a relationship we might find ourselves playing "grin and bear it." It is a powerful practice to learn to relax and accept more and more of the things in life that irritate and upset us. But to simply try to survive it, to wait it out, or to suffer through it will do no good. That is a practice of surviving—and that we already know how to do.

Instead, we first need to recognize tolerance is not serving us in the long run. Then we need to look for ways to help us back off from the place where we tend to go into reaction, defense, or protection mode.

If we are working beyond our edge in a yoga pose, we back off to a place where the intensity is manageable—a place where we can maintain steadiness of mind without going into tolerance or force. In the same way, if we find ourselves over our edge in life's psychic pose, we need to find ways to come back into a zone where the challenge is still present, but we can still manage to work with it skillfully. That might mean taking a break from a conversation, making a request, initiating another type of action or changing the structure of the relationship in a way that reduces the intensity of what is present. By taking a small step back from the elements of the relationship that are triggering us, we help create an environment where we can relax enough to examine our relationship dynamic objectively. From that place we are more likely to be able to make some changes. And, we are also in a better position to be able to let go and accept what cannot be changed.

Sometimes a situation is non-negotiable. There is little or nothing that will make it easier to work with. The places where we *can* work at our edge are practice for these big challenges—where there is no negotiating. But if we have learned along the way to expand our capacity to be with life, we are as well-equipped as we can be when truly tested. We find that our denial and anger about situations is shorter and our ability to accept and take appropriate action comes more quickly. We find ourselves capable of letting go in ways we never imagined.

But many people never get to this point. They re-live their non-negotiable reality over and over. They argue with it. They get mad about it or sad about it. The situation may have even passed, but they have not. As a result, they are consigned to a certain hell of reliving an experience over and over in their minds that no longer has any present validity.

In my relationship with Steve, the non-negotiable reality was our differing sex drives. Little to nothing could be done about it. And what could be done had been. Steve did what he could do to the degree he was willing. That was that. This was a psychic pose that allowed no negotiation. And there were only two options—fight or accept. The first is the one most of us tend to explore exhaustively before we finally give up. Eventually, after we've been through every gamut of fighting with reality, we come to option number two, accepting reality as it is. We stop waiting and wishing for things to be different. We see things as they are—and how they are very likely to continue to be. From that realistic perspective, we can begin to make choices for ourselves based on clear, simple facts rather than the dramatized personal story we habitually create around those facts.

CHANGING THE FORM

In my view, a relationship is a form, and was created for a specific purpose. If that form cannot or no longer serves the purpose for which it was created, it has little value besides its curb appeal. It may be time to look at changing the form itself into something that is more useful for everyone involved and helps each individual continue their own growth and personal unfolding.

A good indication is when we find ourselves continuously beyond our ability to relax with the relationship as it is. When we've genuinely practiced, explored all the options, and looked at the true facts, we need to determine if this is the most appropriate posture for ourselves at this time. We need to ask, "Am I able to use this form in a way that serves me? Have I done everything I can to help it be?" These answers and the choices vary from person to person. I have seen people practice with "non-negotiable" realities nearly impossible in someone else's book. There is no right or wrong. It is simply a question of what will ultimately serve each of us as individuals, and what will not.

Marriage is a form meant to serve us. But many of us end up serving it. We preserve a form for the sake of the form. But the spirit and purpose for which it was created is gone. It is an empty shell. Many of us ignore this because it doesn't fit our picture. We have learned that people shouldn't get divorced. They should stay married no matter what. Marriage is holy. Marriage is forever. Marriage is and was created to be all those things. But if it is not serving the purpose for which it was created, the spirit has already left the construct.

Steve and I were together for ten years. For ten years I played out every scenario I have described here–good and bad. That is not to say that our relationship was only bad times. There were beautiful and wonderful times. But more and more those were overshadowed by my own suppressed needs, which would not be ignored.

CHAPTER TWELVE

IN THE MEANTIME, I had not seen nor heard from Daren since my family had left the yoga center years before. Most of the people I thought were my friends had turned away from my family. I simply could not bear the thought that Daren might be one of them. From time to time I would think about and wonder what had become of him.

I began having a recurring dream in which Daren came to Holland to teach a workshop. As the internet became more and more popular, my dreams prompted me to find him online and eventually I sent him an email to say hello. He responded, but very formally, wishing me and my family well. Mildly disappointed in his lack of enthusiasm, I dismissed it and continued on with life.

A few months later I decided at the spur of the moment to visit my parents, who were now living in Pennsylvania. My brother had purchased a house in which they could live. They had sold a portion of the old yoga center and used one of the remaining buildings to give small seminars. Back to their roots, my mother was once again cooking meals for guests, my father was teaching morning, afternoon and evening, and my brother handled all the administration, housing and marketing.

As I arrived at my parent's home, I quickly took up my usual spot, splayed out on the sofa. My father was sitting and watching TV. I looked over to see what he was watching when a stack of magazines on the coffee table caught my eye. The face staring back at me on the cover of the first magazine was unmistakable. Daren. I turned to look more closely. Was I seeing this right? I sat up and looked at the first cover, then the next one and the next. They were all of Daren. Some were articles, others were covers. I couldn't believe it. I didn't know he had become so well-known.

"That's Daren," my dad said.

"Yes," I replied, with as much nonchalance as I could muster. "Have you heard from him lately?"

"Yes," he replied. My heart jumped. "As a matter of fact, he's coming tomorrow." What?! I couldn't believe it! How could this be happening? Had I heard this right?

As it turned out my father had not heard from Daren since he had left the yoga center. Not one word. Then out of the blue, he called two days earlier and said he wanted to see my father. He was on his way down from Massachusetts. During the only two weeks of the year I was visiting my parents, Daren had called and was coming to visit.

I was excited and fearful at the same time. What would happen? Would the spark still be there? Things were different now. I did not live in a place where my every move was constantly watched. My father had long since trusted me to find my own way in the world. He would not be acting the part of the protective father of my youth. Of course nothing untoward would happen. I was married, and I loved Steve. But it would give us the opportunity I hoped for, to finally talk to each other.

True to form, Daren did not arrive on time. He was a day late. By then I had been on pins and needles for over twenty-four hours, and the wait was excruciating. Finally word came, they had arrived. They? More than one? I had to find a reason to get over to the seminar building where he was staying.

For the first time in my life, I volunteered to do the laundry as the machines were in the seminar building. Loaded with bags of dirty laundry I walked down the cement path, trying to appear relaxed as my eyes surreptitiously scanned for any sign of him. Nothing. I walked upstairs and put in the first load. Still nothing. Then I heard voices in my brother's living room. He lived in the seminar building as well. I approached the living room, my breath almost non-existent. The anticipation was killing me. I didn't hear Daren's voice. I navigated the corner and took in the room before anyone noticed me.

He was not there, but two other people were—a man and a woman. I greeted them both. I knew the man, but who was the woman? She was very attractive. Was she Daren's girlfriend? My mind immediately kicked-in as I carried on polite conversation. If she was his girlfriend, I'd have to keep my distance. We would not be able to talk. My hopes were dashed. I soon found out that Daren had gone to sleep and that he would be joining the group for our morning yoga practice. I would have to wait yet another day.

The next morning I dressed carefully. Almost sixteen years had passed since we'd first met, but that same feeling of wanting to wear just the right thing, to make just the right impression, came back to me instantly. Through bits of information gathered from snippets of conversation, I found Daren was not in a relationship with his attractive female companion.

The night before, I had called Steve to tell him what was happening. We told each other everything, and this was no exception. Sensing my excitement and anxiety, he told me to relax, be open and be myself. He encouraged me not to be fearful or standoffish just because we were married. He trusted me to do what was right for me, and for us, and this gave me trust in myself.

Armed with Steve's support, I made my way to the meditation room. I stepped in and immediately sensed Daren looking at me. I greeted various people, and as I did, felt the intensity of his gaze follow my every movement, every gesture and every expression.

Finally, when my eyes turned to meet his, the spark was there. No denying it. We hugged, but said little besides perfunctory remarks. The unspoken communication was an acknowledgement of what had once been, but now could no longer be in the same form. We would put the past behind us and simply allow that spark to be channeled into an open, easy friendship.

Daren spent the rest of the morning teaching us the ins and outs of a unique, acrobatic style of yoga he had developed. We all had a wonderful time, but throughout the weekend there was never an opportunity for us to create any closure to the past. We had ended our relationship years before on the phone, but not spoken since, and I let go of the idea. What happened was the best that could, and I would trust it.

About an hour before Daren was to leave, I went to say my goodbyes. It was finally time to stop trying, to let go and move on. I walked into the room where Daren, his friends, and my brother were sitting.

Alice, his friend, turned to me and said, "Daren is scheduled to come to Amsterdam to teach a workshop, but his sponsor has become very ill. Would you be willing to take over?" My mind jumped to the recurring dream in which he was coming to Holland.

"Sure," I replied. "I'd be happy to help." I didn't know how Steve would feel, but I didn't know what else to say.

Saying goodbye, I hugged each of our guests. In our short time together we had developed a nice bond. Daren was last.

I wanted my hug to communicate all I felt but could not say, but didn't dare let down my guard in front of the others. "I'm sorry we didn't have a chance to talk this time," I said. "Maybe next time I see you."

He jumped on my words, "Well, we can talk right now. Let's go outside."

We made our way outside to a picnic table, still within view of his friends. We sat in silence, neither of us knowing what to say or where to begin, and then started with small talk.

"How did you end up in Holland? How did the two of you meet?" he asked.

"We're in Holland mostly because my husband is Dutch," I replied, smiling.

"Oh," he laughed. "I guess that's a good reason."

Our eyes met and our discomfort began to dissipate.

I briefly outlined the story of Steve. I could tell he was curious, but also did not want too much information.

He paused for a moment, hesitating.

"The last time I saw you I didn't know you were married. I couldn't understand why no one had told me. I was stunned. Even though it didn't work out for us all those years before, I thought it eventually would. I thought you would wait for me. When I came back and found out you were married, I couldn't believe it. I guess our timing was off."

I was thoroughly taken aback. When Daren and I parted ways no mention was made of a possible future. It never occurred to me he'd even thought of it, though of course I had. Then the words fell out of my mouth.

"I love Steve," I said. "And I'm happy with him. I'm committed to being with him. But I love you, too. It may not make sense, but that is the way it is. I love you, and I can't change that either."

Daren nodded. The feelings were there, but reality had taken another turn. They could be acknowledged, even allowed to exist, but no action could ever be taken.

"People ask me why I haven't remarried," he said, his eyes softening into shades of melancholy as he looked past my shoulder. "I tell them I've been waiting for my Indian princess."

I was deeply touched. I wanted so much to lean over and hold him closely, but the giant divide of our past, my present, and the faces looking down at us from above kept me stiffly in my place seated across from him.

Abruptly, he changed the tone of the conversation. It had gone too deep and become too uncomfortable.

We shifted back to my life in Holland, his blossoming career, and began to walk back. Though careful not to touch, in our hearts we were arm-in-arm. I told him I always knew he would rise to the top. With his presence and charisma it was a sure thing.

He opened the door, and as I stepped through, it closed on our past. We immediately dropped behind the mask of old acquaintances, neither of us wanting to show how deeply the feelings ran. The group speculatively watched us but we didn't reveal a thing. We had been trained to hide from curious eyes.

His friends had packed the car and were ready to leave. Daren said his goodbyes to my brother and the rest of the group. Finally, it was only me. For this one moment, our last, we both allowed ourselves to completely let down our guards. If anyone had been watching closely, they would have seen naked emotion on both of our faces. We were open and vulnerable to the world and each other. He opened his arms and I stepped into them. For a few seconds we allowed our hearts to show what we really felt. Or bodies melted into each other. The walls separating us dissolved into a temporary union. Then, as if by design, we both stepped away from each other at the exact same moment. Both of us turned away as if nothing had happened, not even making eye contact. After the hug we shared, anything but a quick disconnection would have been too obvious.

I watched from an upper story window as he followed his friends out the front door. I made no effort to hide. Sensing my gaze, he turned to look at me once more. He stopped, looked straight at me and put his hand over his heart, saying nothing. He just stood there looking at me. I smiled back, my own hand over my heart, laughing delightedly.

He gave me one last nod before turning to walk towards the car. Several times he turned to look back at me. Each time I was standing there, and I stayed until after they had driven away. I wanted to imprint this memory in my mind forever.

It was true what I had said. I did love Daren. But I also loved Steve. And Steve was the one I had chosen to be with. Eventually, I slowly turned away from the window. I had an incredibly rich and rewarding relationship with Steve. Though lacking in some areas, it was more than many could hope for in others. Less than a week later, I was back in Holland and my life continued as before.

CHAPTER THIRTEEN

WHILE I LOVED Steve deeply, I continued to feel resentful my needs were not being met. But the resentment was not logical. It rarely is. I began to see him as an obstacle to my happiness. Of course this was not true. I chose to stay with him, and in doing so ignored my needs. I resented *him* for the fact I had not listened to myself. In effect, I held him responsible for my not honoring myself. But it was my doing.

Nevertheless, resentment would arise more and more often. Like veils being slowly peeled back to reveal the stark clarity of reality, I began to see that after ten years, maybe he wasn't going to change. It became apparent in stages, like waking from a deep sleep. Short glimpses brought on a slow but steady realization that what I thought was going to be would never happen. This was it. There would be no fairytale ending. I would not ride off into the sunset with my happily ever after. This was exactly how it was going to be for the rest of our married life.

Now one might think it was obvious from the beginning, and it was. But we have a funny way of taking the truth and softening it with our fantasy of how it could be different in the future. It's called hope. And I used it to cope with the parts of reality I could not deal with in the present moment.

Not to say hope is all bad. If a friend were depressed, I'd want them to have hope. But it kept me hanging on to a future that did not exist. I used hope to keep me going, though it was clear from the very beginning Steve was not going to change.

At one point, Steve and I decided on a vacation in Crete. We arrived on a small secluded beach, with only four small apartments, traditional chalk white walls, bright blue windows and fuchsia-colored flowers overflowing from beams overhanging the deck. The view from our bedroom was powder blue sky touching a sapphire ocean, an empty golden beach welcoming us.

We spent our days swimming, walking and exploring the island. But I hoped for more. I hoped somehow the vacation would magically change things, and Steve would suddenly find me irresistible. But it was not to be. He was perfectly happy with how we were and had no need to change anything. If I pressed, he withdrew. If I let go, we could enjoy ourselves. Hope waned.

Clarity, that had already begun to dawn, was now becoming more and more evident. It was not going to get better or be different. I had spent ten years hoping, waiting, and wishing for change, and I had a choice to make. But first I had to give up hope. I had to acknowledge I had been trying to soften the cold reality with a rosier future. I had to let go of fantasy and look at the facts.

WHERE ARE YOU?

My wise father once told me, "You can only begin your journey from where you are." In my hopes of change for the future, I had not acknowledged the truth of where I was now. Because of that, my journey could not begin.

When we are lost and call a friend for help the first question they will ask is "Where are you?" Without this vital piece of information, we are unable to take the next steps to get to where we need to go. In my case, I was unwilling to acknowledge where I was. I was unwilling to fully accept the truth of my situation. To put myself back on the path, this was the first thing I had to do; tell the truth about where I was. Only then could I begin to make any progress towards figuring out what direction my life needed to take.

I realized acceptance doesn't necessarily mean giving in to the way things are. It means allowing for the fact this is the reality of the way things are right now. Then, from that clarity of knowing objectively where we stand on the map, we can decide where we need to go.

WOULD IT HAVE BEEN BETTER IF...?

Once we accept the reality of where we are, we often second guess our original choices. A thousand times I have asked myself whether I should have decided not to marry Steve all those years ago. Would it have been better if I had not hoped, stayed out of the relationship, and moved on with my life with someone else? My head says, "maybe," but my heart says, "no way." Despite everything we went through, I know it was exactly as it should have been. I needed to be with Steve. We grew up together. Regardless of the outcome, we learned how to truly love outside of conventional forms or structures. The gifts of the experience were not solely in the end result, but in the value of the process we went through. I had to trust that whatever happened, whether the "goal" was reached or not, it was exactly what needed to happen for me to learn the lessons I needed to learn. We learned how to love each other unconditionally, yet still honor who we are as individuals. We truly loved. We still do. And I would not trade the experience I had with him for anything. It was the most significant experience of my life and I still feel to this day that he was God's greatest gift to me.

Had I dismissed the intrinsic value of the process, I might have overlooked all that. I might have dismissed ten years of my life, called it a failure and moved on without taking its gifts with me.

GROWING MY OWN TREE

As I began to truly see I could not count on Steve to be any different than he was, I began to shift my attention back to myself. I started to grow my own tree; developing my own friendships and social life. If Steve didn't want to go out dancing, I went with my girlfriends. I stopped trying to please him and started to please myself. I started to become a happier person in my own right and began to climb out of the hole I had created for myself. I saw I was a valuable person in my own right who did not need to look to anyone to give me my sense of self worth.

As I did this, the weight started coming off. I didn't even really try. It just didn't fit me anymore. For the first time in six years, I dropped below 200 pounds. I never believed I would see that day again, but here it was.

I began to realize no one person could ever hope to fulfill my needs. To put that burden on anyone else was to put a load on the relationship that could eventually break the back of the very real bonds we shared. All Steve wanted was to be himself and love me the way he loved me. It was not his responsibility to make me happy. It was mine. If my needs weren't met, it was my job to make sure they were, through my connections with various people and life experiences.

In order to do that, I had to open myself up to the world. I could no longer exist in a little bubble in which everyone besides Steve was subtly relegated to second place. I had to let people in and share myself fully. If I gave myself fully to my life, life would be given back to me. This realization brought me out of my hiding place in relationships. And the result showed in my body and in my developing friendships.

RELATIONSHIPS NATURALLY MATURE

Over time as a relationship develops, it changes. It tends to move from the other person being the limit of our universe to including them as a central character in the larger scope of our lives. Each has their own life. Those lives intertwine in certain important ways. New experiences and interactions serve closeness, rather than detracting from it. The continued input keeps the relationship exciting and interesting.

Many of us resist this change. We think it is a sign the relationship is over. But even in relationship we are meant to bloom on our own, to grow our own tree, to uniquely express who we are and share that uniqueness with another. Instead, the idea many of us hold is that a relationship should mean the end of our individuality. We give up on growing our own tree. We may even attempt to get rid of our individuality in an effort to create closeness. When that stage naturally falls away and we are called back into a natural expression of who we are, we may imagine something is wrong. We think things should always be the way they were in the beginning. We may even try to go back to recreate the past only to find its time has passed.

But perhaps, it is this new phase that affords us the most opportunity to grow as individuals. To find our own joy, happiness and unique expression in the world while having a beloved companion to share that with. If allowed to be, this new phase can bring an invaluable depth to the relationship and greater expansiveness to each individual life.

Of course, this greater autonomy needs to be combined with a willful practice of keeping the primary connection alive. Sometimes we go to the other extreme. Each individual is so wrapped up in their own lives, career, social life and responsibilities they lose touch with the other. Without realizing it, partners continue to share a bed but little else, essentially living alongside one another without intersecting at essential points. This is where it takes willful and deliberate attention to keep the relationship alive and dynamic, while still attending to individual responsibilities. Often it is left to one person to keep the connection alive.

It Isn't Fair

This doesn't always seem fair. It is easy to interpret that the partner is not as invested because they do not take the initiative. The mind wants to say, "They don't love me as much as I love them." Or, "If they don't take the initiative, why should I?" In some ways fairness is a social construct. It is based on the idea that things should operate as an even exchange. We give to get. We often take that idea into relationship and find ourselves sorely disappointed when the exchange we are expecting is not forthcoming.

Consider the love we are speaking about is not exchange-based. It is about learning to give from the fullness of who we are because we want to—because it makes us feel good to do it. We get the benefit not from the reaction or validation we get from the other, but from the act of letting what is inside us be shared fully with another. We give to give. We all know what this feels like. When truly practiced, nothing in this world is more fulfilling. It exists far beyond the paradigm of exchange.

That is not to say significant imbalances in a relationship should not be addressed. But address those issues not by withholding love, but by stating the request while maintaining an open stance to the other. Sometimes we use what we perceive as lack of "fairness" as a reason to withhold–until the other person measures up to our expectations. Many of us end up withholding for a very long time because we never get our expectations of fairness met. Ultimately, we are the ones who suffer. Every time we close down, we hurt ourselves before we hurt anyone else.

In the end the question is, "Am I more dedicated to fairness, or to keeping the relationship alive?" What is more important is what serves the common connection between both individuals.

This also shows up when we are convinced we are right and the other is wrong. One could argue I was "right" that Steve should have sex with me. On the other hand, he could have argued I should not force him to be other than who he was. He would be "right," too. Each of us could get into our camps and justify why the other is wrong and we are in the right. But it would not get us any closer to love.

Someone once told me, "Being right is the booby prize." We end up being right but losing the very thing we wanted in the first place–love, connection, happiness and peace. We make ourselves unhappy, angry and frustrated because our "rightness" is not acknowledged by the one who is "wrong." But being right is unlikely to get the other person to change. More likely, it will make them defensive and distance them all the more. Our question to ourselves is, "Do I want to be right or do I want an open heart?" If we give in to our desire to be right, our happiness is held hostage by the mind's desire to win. If we let connection be more important than being right, we are cultivating heart and togetherness over winning and losing.

CHAPTER FOURTEEN

O NE DAY, returning home to Holland after leading a corporate yoga retreat, I received a phone call. Alice, Daren's friend whom I had met in Pennsylvania, still wanted me to help put together a workshop for him in Amsterdam. The original sponsor had never fully recovered from her illness, so I said I'd be willing to help. I found a space, marketed to the students at our studio, placed ads and articles in magazines and put up flyers around town, largely at my own cost. Though I had Steve's support, he was not thrilled to see the amount of time, energy and money I was putting into making this workshop a success. It was clear I had more investment in this event than the average workshop.

When I had last seen Daren, he and Alice were not in-volved. This time, when I picked them up from the airport it was clear something more had developed. Thankfully, I had al-ready put myself in "professional" mode, so my friendly distance was already firmly in place as they came out of customs hand-in-hand, bodies subtly leaning into each other in the knowing comfort of lovers. Distancing myself by playing the tour guide, I showed them where to change money and buy train tickets. As we made our way into the city, Daren asked about Steve. How was he? Was he going to be at home? I assured him Steve would be home later, after work.

That night, after a day of sightseeing and showing Daren and Alice around the city, Steve came home. It was all I could do not to jump into the comfort of his arms. How ironic was it that I was seeking solace for a past that had never happened, with my present husband? Once Steve was there I could relax and let him carry the conversation. He already knew what I would be feeling and as the gentleman that he was, he not only didn't make it worse, he ran interference for me. Luckily, Steve and Daren hit it off beautifully. I could see the light of grudging respect come into Steve's eyes. That night, Steve and I went off to our bedroom. Alice and Daren went off to theirs. I could not have imagined a more bizarre scenario, yet I had managed to create it and now had to live through it.

As the days before the workshop passed, Alice and Daren did more and more of their own thing. I would take them shopping or to a local market, but it was clear that Alice did not feel comfortable with my interacting with Daren. I was not sure if he had told her about our old connection or if she simply remembered the way Daren and I had said goodbye the last time we'd met. In any case, it didn't matter. I backed off as much as possible, only speaking directly to Daren when etiquette required I do so.

This was quite the situation I'd gotten myself into. I'd have to give more thought to the ramifications before I said yes to things like this in the future.

"Note to self," I thought. "Do not organize workshops for old flames while married." Though I had certainly adopted the European ethic of being able to let go of the past and be friends with exes and their new girlfriends, this was a bit over the top for me. Almost comical. And we weren't done yet.

Thankfully Steve had a day off and we all went biking in the countryside. As we passed grazing sheep, goats and cows, we set ourselves up at the base of a small hillock for a bite and some partner yoga along the way. No one else was to be seen. Steve and Daren were still getting along famously. I took a picture of the two of them smiling for the camera. Bit by bit I was acclimatizing to this new twist reality had taken. It was as if everything that had come before had never been. It was a lot easier if I just left it that way and allowed myself to enjoy the present, free of the story that had come before it.

Moments later, as we arranged ourselves back onto our bikes, Daren pulled up behind me to wait while I adjusted my seat. Finished, I looked up at him inquiringly. I had the impression he had something he wanted to say.

"Beautiful view," he said.

"Yes," I replied. "It's very pretty. I love it here."

"Now our paths have gone in different directions," he said haltingly. "We each have our own lives. The time for what we had has passed."

"Yes," I replied, and as I said it I did not feel sad or regretful. It was simply the truth.

We smiled at each other, got on our bikes and caught up to Steve and Alice.

That weekend Daren gave the workshop and Alice assisted. It was a rousing success. Happy, we all went home, but Steve had to work so I made dinner for Daren and Alice. It was a very nice evening and I was enjoying myself. Daren took out a CD of Rumi poetry that a number of his clients in the Hollywood scene had teamed together to create. The poetry was read by the recognizable voices of various stars and was set to subtle strains of sitar music in the background. Then a piece of poetry came on that struck the center of my heart. The line was something like, "The moment our eyes met, my soul knew yours… I saw your face and I knew you were the one." Those words transported me back to the memory of my first meeting with Daren all those years ago. The moment when our eyes first met and my soul knew his. My heart burst open. Tears rose in my eyes. All the feelings I had reasoned away came flooding back in an uncontrollable instant. Daren and Alice, oblivious of my state, continued to listen to the poetry intently. Quietly, I rose.

"Please stay and listen. I'm going to bed," I said softly, implying I was exhausted, maybe feeling a little sick. They nodded and I left quietly.

I dove under the covers, creating a little cave for myself where I could find a measure of space, a place to feel what I felt without having to edit or talk myself out of anything. As I stared into the dark space of my makeshift cave, hot tears began to roll silently down my cheeks, my mind temporarily suspended. No thoughts, no memories. Just a deep ache in my heart that finally demanded to be felt. After a time, I fell asleep. When Steve came home an hour or two later, I awoke. In a sleepy, childlike voice I asked him to hold me. He held me in his arms and together we fell asleep.

The next morning, Steve and I lay in bed and talked for a while until we heard Daren and Alice shuffling about in the kitchen. Steve and I always told each other everything, so I gave him an inkling of what had happened the night before. I knew this couldn't be easy for him either, and there was no point in making it worse by going into too many details. In any case, it was my issue to work out.

Steve went out to greet our guests, and he left for work shortly after. As a massage therapist and yoga teacher I had the liberty of shifting clients and finding substitute teachers when necessary, so I was able to stay. After Steve left, Alice got in the shower. I busied myself in the kitchen putting away dishes. Daren came in, silently leaning back on the kitchen counter to watch me.

In a soft tone he asked, "Why were you crying last night?"

Startled into honesty I replied, "How did you know I was crying? I didn't make a sound."

"I felt you crying," he replied in a low voice as if gentling an anxious mare.

I stared at him mutely, my hands awkwardly wielding kitchen utensils I had been putting away. There was nothing I could say this time. As he had said, the time for us had passed and there was no going back.

Finally, after what seemed like an interminable pause, I managed to come up with, "I'm working through some stuff with Steve, but nothing out of the ordinary."

Daren nodded understandingly. He said a few words about relationships and how they took constant willingness to attend to daily irritations. He was right, but in this case, he had no way of knowing what was really happening couldn't have been further from the mark.

I smiled and thanked him, my eyes not quite courageous enough to reach his. His eyes gently caught and held mine. He smiled into my eyes. No words, but an acknowledgement of the connection we had once allowed ourselves to share.

CHAPTER FIFTEEN

At the end of the week, Daren and Alice returned home. Steve and I settled back into the rhythm of our lives and soon the drama of their visit faded from memory. I continued to unearth a renewed sense of vitality through my work, my life and began investing time and attention in close friendships.

As I came into my own, I began to look at Steve less and less through my hopes and dreams of who he might someday become. I began to look at him just as he was right now. I noticed myself being a kind of detective. Instead of seeing Steve through the filter of who I had made him out to be, I began to see him just as he was. No more, no less. I wanted to see him free of my hopes and my dreams. Just him. Right now. Before, I could not allow myself to do this. True seeing might mean I would leave him, and that was the one thing I could not allow to happen. Now I was willing to face it all and be open to it. I could allow myself to see all sides of the relationship, not with judgment, but a sense of curiosity.

To my surprise, what emerged was an overwhelming sense of love, a deep sense of allowing for who he was, and a deep appreciation of it. What had masked this love before was my need for him to be different. When I could let that go, even for a moment, I was able to see him as he was. I had not allowed myself to do this fully in the past because I was afraid that acceptance meant having to live with no sex. Now I began to see another way. Acceptance of Steve was just the first step. It did not mean I had to stay with him. It was simply a way of coming into alignment with reality, then making my life choices from there. Acceptance did not mean the end of me; it was the beginning of making choices that served me.

Soon the conscious practice of letting go of conditions started to become natural and effortless. More and more I loved Steve for who he was. My resentment, my expectations of us as a perfect couple, fell away. But I also began to realize it did not mean I needed to stay in the relationship in the current form. The form of the relationship might need to change—or it might not. But I needed to be open to all possibilities. Acceptance also meant accepting who I was and what my needs were. I had to determine if the relationship in its current manifestation was beyond my capability of relaxing with it.

Was I just tolerating the situation rather than truly learning to expand my capacity to accept reality? Was there a way I could back off my edge to make the relationship more doable, so I could stay in it, in its current form? These questions began to surface once I made that first step.

My relationship with Steve continued on for another year. My life continued to flower in other directions. But the core issues did not shift. My desire to have my needs met did not diminish. In fact, the more I came into my own, the stronger that voice became.

Though I had made many strides in accepting the situation, developing a full life and learning to love Steve as he was, I was still not acknowledging my own need to know a passionate sexual relationship. It became clear that all the things I got from Steve, as important as they were, could not cover up listening to my own needs.

I not only began to see the truth of who Steve was, but also the truth of who I was. Part of me was simply living with the way things were because it was easier and less scary than taking the steps to change it. There were so many good things about the relationship I did not want to let go of. And it was easier to stay with something that was half-working than fully commit to the unknown.

I needed to back off my edge to a place where I could truly feel married to Steve versus trying to hold on because it was safer than moving on.

One day Steve and I sat down at our dining table. In the next few days I would be leaving for the States to visit my parents. It was clear to me how I needed to back off of my edge in the relationship. It was quite simple. While I didn't require he change his sexual attitudes overnight, I did want some effort on his part to look at himself, to see any issues which, when dealt with, could create a shift in our sexual relationship. Bottom line: I wanted willingness. If there were a willingness on Steve's part to look at his own issues, it would allow me to relax more with the way the relationship was. I would know there was intent for movement in a certain direction. Though there was no guarantee anything would change, just knowing this would make my staying in the form of the relationship doable. Though we had tried this avenue before, I had not spoken it with clarity and conviction. This time was different.

"What are you going to do in the States?" he asked.

"I'm going to visit my parents, and some friends as well," I replied.

"Steve I need you to think about something while I'm gone. I want you to consider taking some concrete steps to resolve this issue between us. For me, that means us seeing a therapist, but you might have other ideas as well. Would you give that some serious thought? After I come back we can discuss it and decide what to do from there."

Now, in hindsight, it needs to be said I could have gone to a therapist on my own. I had taken half-hearted attempts at therapies, various workshops, and individual counseling sessions, but in all fairness I did not give it the kind of dedication I gave to the idea of us doing therapy together. I was still dedicated to the idea we *both* had to change. Now that it is so clear how much of what I experienced was a reflection of my own inner world, pursuing more internal insight would have been an obvious answer. But at the time, it didn't occur to me. In my mind, it was about him, and now I have learned differently. I have seen many relationships in which one person has courageously made internal changes, and changed their experience of the relationship as a result. I did not learn that one this time around.

Steve agreed to give it some thought. I felt relieved and empowered just through the act of taking action towards a form of relationship that would be workable for me. I had done the willful part of making my request. Now, my only job was to accept the answer and make my choices.

A month later I returned to Amsterdam. I found myself sitting at the same seat at the dining table, Steve across from me. Coming home from the airport we were happy to see each other and greeted each other with our usual genuine affection. We had deliberately refrained from going directly to the unspoken question hanging in the air. Now, at the table once again, our conversation settled into the reality of the moment.

"Did you have some time to think about my request?" I asked.

"Yes," Steve replied. "I did give it a lot of thought."

"Are you willing to do therapy with me?"

"No. I love you very much Kamini. You are the love of my life. But right now, I have to accept myself as I am. I'm no longer willing to do anything to change myself that comes from judgment rather than self-acceptance. I'm sorry if that hurts or disappoints you, but I have to stick with myself."

As I listened to Steve, I heard him clearly. Not through my wants or wishes. Not through blame or hope. Just what he was telling me. I could see his point of view clearly. I understood. I would have liked it to have been different, but it was not. Steve was who he was. He needed to do and be how he needed to be. How could I blame him, when that was exactly what I was seeking to do myself?

I nodded silently. My heart was filled with love and understanding, not only for him but also for myself. I was filled with clarity and a kind of peace. I had all the information I needed to make my choices.

"I get it," I said. "I really do. And, given that, I can't be in this relationship any more. I have gone as far as I can go with things the way they are. If I stayed longer my feelings of resentment would take over my life and I don't want that. I feel like my spirit would die. I would be alive but I would be dead inside." I went on to explain if I stayed in the form of the relationship as it was, I would just be going through the motions because that is what is expected, but in the process I would be denying myself a life that is in alignment with who I am and my own self-expression.

Steve nodded his head in understanding. He understood my position as well. How could he quarrel with that?

Our conversation was surprisingly short and equable. We got up and began to cook dinner together. We knew something monumental had shifted. It was as if the one thing neither of us wanted to confront–the possibility of a life without the other– had finally been faced. Instead of fear, we felt the weight of that fear released from our shoulders. Now we could be free to enjoy each other exactly as we were, without the burden of trying to be different.

In the weeks to follow, Steve and I found a sense of love and enjoyment of each other we had not felt since the very first years we were together. All expectations had been erased. We could just enjoy each other as we were without needing something different. Of course, the question came up in our minds if we really needed to break up. Things were going so well. Why had we not done this before? All we had done was completely release each other from the need to be different.

But then we came back to reality of where we were. Nothing had changed in terms of our basic wants and needs in the relationship. No, it was clear that the form of the relationship we had created–marriage–with the norms that came with it, no longer fit us. The form of our relationship clearly needed to change to match who we could now be for each other. Steve could not be my lover, but he could continue to be my best friend, my confidant, my family. I could continue to love Steve just as he was, provide a listening and accepting ear, but not in the form of marriage that carried the promise of physical closeness with it.

And so this is how we came upon the big "D" of divorce. We chose to see it as ending a form through which we loved rather than ending the love itself. Others might say this was simply a way to whitewash the enormity of our choice. I cannot say which is true. But I can say that still to this day, we carry on our vows in certain ways. He is still the closest person to me in my life. He knows me at my best and at my worst and accepts it all. He is my family and I would do anything for him that I would do for my blood family. For me, we changed the form of our relationship, and that is what allowed the love we had to continue to live on.

At the divorce, our lawyer said he had never seen such an amicable parting of ways, and wished it could be like that for everyone. We simply looked at each other and smiled.

CHAPTER SIXTEEN

THIS IS NOT to say I advocate divorce as the only option when things are at a breaking point. I know many people I admire deeply who have held on through these kinds of challenges and come out the better for it. They continued to grow as individuals within the form of their relationship, and their relationship and love have become stronger and deeper as a result. They are the example of what a relationship can be when used as a practice. However, changing form, letting go and moving on is an often less-acknowledged cousin, and can be equally valid. There is no one right way for everyone. That is for each person to determine on their own based on their use of relationship as a form and the boundaries and limitations within which they are able to practice.

To Deny the Past is to Deny the Path that Brought Us Here

When we make either of these choices, it is easy to doubt ourselves. "Should I have gotten out?" Or "Could I have made it through if I had just hung on a little longer?" Then we come up with all the reasons to justify our decision, or perhaps put ourselves down for the choice we made. In the end, it comes down to one thing. We did what we did. It already happened. Thinking about how it could have been handled better is wasting energy on something that cannot be changed. The only question now is if we want to continue to rehash a choice made long ago or accept that no matter how pretty or ugly, this was our path.

Our path is meant to bring us to where we are. The way we can make the best use of the path we chose is by looking objectively at what worked and what didn't as we traveled, taking what we learned from that journey and moving on. To regret the past is to regret the path that brought us to where we are.

The path is the only passage by which we each uniquely arrive at where we are now. To deny the way we got here is to deny all that we have learned and achieved through the course of our lives. If we had not had all the life experiences we've had, would we be the same person? Would we have the same wisdom and insight? Would we be as mature as we are? My guess is not.

No amount of reading books or taking workshops can replace the lessons learned through real-life experience. I grew up in a community where I learned many of the teachings of the east as a child. But that could not spare me from having to learn my own life lessons. Parents with the benefit and insight of experience cannot save their children from their own painful lessons. No matter how much anyone appears to know, no one is exempt. To imagine that any one of us can somehow get through life without muddying ourselves with humanity is unrealistic. It is what we are doing here.

Social Purpose v. Spiritual Purpose of Relationship

For most of us, we have learned marriage is something we should stay in for a lifetime. It should last forever, and if it doesn't it is considered a failure. I suspect the original purpose of marriage and the one I'm outlining here are more in line with each other than we might think.

The purpose of the form of marriage is commitment. Marriage is most effective when it creates transformational pressure. It has to box us in to effectively bring up issues through which we learn about ourselves. If we felt we could get out at any time, it would not serve its purpose as a place to practice meeting intensity and discomfort with greater equanimity and balance. The only way to be boxed in is to set parameters. Marriage vows outline the parameters of the box. Only then do we have a true form with transformational potential within which to practice.

However, this concept can easily become dogmatic. The idea of marriage and the vows that shape it can take on a life of their own, becoming stronger and more important than the health and well-being of the individuals that make it up. Then, instead of marriage serving the growth of the people in it, the individuals begin to serve the form.

THE PURPOSE OF VOWS

The form of a relationship is comparable to the form of a yoga pose. In a pose, we are asked to adhere to certain alignment cues such as, "Move your hands towards your toes." In marriage it might be, "Love and accept your partner in sickness and in health." We will all have greater or lesser degrees of success with this. But success at touching the toes is not the point. The point is to move towards what is asked of us, and then watch our habitual patterns and fears come up. In a yoga class we might try to push past our own limits towards the toes. In a relationship we might do the same. Or, we might do just the opposite. Out of fear, we might completely withdraw. We might want to run away with the weight of the pressure we feel when a loved one is suddenly ill.

The truth is, very few people will actually take all their vows, the alignment cues of the pose called marriage, and be able to execute them perfectly. And that is not necessarily the purpose. Instead the purpose is to move to the best of one's ability towards the alignment cues of the form called marriage.

The vows we make to each other are places within which we can study who we are. Rather than ideals many of us try to force ourselves to live up to, it may be helpful to think of them as contexts within which we study who we are. Some of these contexts in relationship are: faithfulness, commitment, honesty, and willingness to face both ups and downs together. In some areas we may find we are strong and have no problem practicing the alignment cues. In others, we may find old insecurities and fears surfacing.

A common one for men and women, for example, is a fear of commitment. A fear of being tied down. One way to look at this would be to say that a person has to have no fears about being in relationship before entering into one. Another way to look at it would be to use the relationship as *an opportunity to learn about the fear of losing one's freedom.* One avenue creates an idea that we have to be perfect. Very few of us, if anyone, can live up to that. The other allows for each person to be who they are and use the relationship as a place within which to learn about themselves.

This is not to say that "anything goes," for it is unlikely most partners will allow their significant other to "learn" about faithfulness within the parameters of a relationship, nor am I saying they should. But, if or when something like this should happen, it may be useful to look at the situation as something for both parties to learn from in the context of faithfulness rather than just pointing to the broken vows and calling the entire venture a failure.

And, should that form someday need to end or change, rather than thinking of vows as something that failed, we might notice how they may be reworked to fit the new way we have chosen to relate. If we are divorced and share children for example, that new relationship may have its own "vows" or alignment cues that help it be the best relationship it can be. In other words, let the vows, like alignment cues, change to best serve the changing form.

CHAPTER SEVENTEEN

After Steve and I decided to end our marriage, I found a new place to live not far away. He helped me pack up most of my things and move to my new place. After hauling numerous boxes up two flights of stairs and stacking them in the middle of my studio apartment, he said goodbye. I knew I would be seeing him shortly, so I didn't make much of it. Yet, once that door closed, I found myself completely alone for the first time in ten years. The person who had become as much a part of me as myself was no longer there.

Our energies had become inextricably intertwined. Now that we were no longer together I felt as if he was invisibly being torn out of my system. I not only felt deep sadness but physical pain at our parting.

Then, as the days passed, it got easier. I relied heavily on my friends, whom I credit with scooping me up and firmly placing me back into the driver's seat of my own life when I found myself in listless and melancholy moods.

I started wearing high-heeled boots and trendy clothes. I would work with students and clients all day and then go out with my friends to parties, dinners, dancing, and gatherings in the park. It was a painful time, yet freeing at the same time. I had never experienced such a connection to, and reliance upon, a circle of friends in my adult life. I had never really experienced what it was like to go out, to dress up, to feel beautiful and to flirt. It was empowering and healing to experience myself as an attractive woman through the eyes of others.

And slowly, through their belief in me, I began to believe in my own attractiveness again. At the same time there was a certain underlying sense of freneticism, of running on a wheel I could not let myself get off of even for a moment. If I were to let go of my now non-stop life, I would have to go back to feeling the pain of the loss I had incurred.

Once, late at night, I was biking along the Prinsengracht, one of the main canals in the center of Amsterdam. The lights glowed softly across the water, apartments lit, cozy interiors accessible to my curious eyes. I looked into the apartments remembering how Steve and I would take our nightly walks into the city, gazing into these apartments, hoping and dreaming for the day when we would have our own. All the time we had been together in Amsterdam, we had had to sublet apartments due to the housing crunch. As I turned my gaze once again in front of me, I saw Steve on his bike coming towards me. By that time, our divorce papers had been finalized. We still saw each other now and then, but usually others were around and conversation was limited to more superficial levels.

We both recognized each other simultaneously, though we had both changed quite a bit. I was slimmer; my hair was cut fashionably short. Steve, always conscious of dressing well, had taken his fashion sense to a new level. Hip shoes, lightly distressed jeans, form-fitting t-shirt and disheveled hair completed his look. Upon seeing each other, we both lit up, smiles erupting on our faces.

'Hi Steve!" I called out.

"Hi Kam!" he smiled, his white teeth shining in the darkness.

We stopped in the middle of the street and gave each other the customary kisses on each cheek. Then we simply looked at each other, silent. So much had passed to bring us to this moment. Just like the water passing on the canal behind us, much had changed, yet that same spark that had once brought us together was still there.

We decided to go a café nearby and chat. Soon we were seated next to one another, talking and catching up. He admired my new look. I admired his. He told me how things were going with his new girlfriend. When they'd first started seeing one another, he'd called to tell me. He is nothing if not forthright. I could always depend on him to tell me the truth. Initially, it was painful. In the way I tend to do with everything, I took it personally. Why could he have with her what he didn't have with me? But God doesn't answer "why" questions. Things just are the way they are. And over time I came to accept it.

This time, as Steve recounted the details of his new relationship, I felt my heart become fuller. In the midst of a sweet pain, I was genuinely happy for him. I knew in that moment what we shared could, and would, co-exist with other relationships that might come and go in our lives. We were forever bound in love and nothing would change that.

The waiter came and we each ordered a glass of wine. We laughed. While we were married I never drank, and Steve rarely. Apparently we'd both changed in this respect. Settling back into our conversation, I asked all the proper questions as he told me about what was going on with his life. Eventually, the conversation turned to me.

"So what is happening with you?" he asked intently.

"I've been going out a bit. It's good for me." I told him about a couple of developing male interests, but he must have felt some hesitation in my voice.

"What is it?" he asked.

"You know, it's really weird. And I really don't know what to make of it. I've been dreaming a lot about Daren. The dream is always the same. I think I probably told you about it even when we were married." Now these same dreams had become more intense and more frequent. They were always a little unsettling, and left me feeling unfinished or incomplete in some way.

As we sat in the café drinking our wine, I described the dream. I was in a large building with many rooms. I knew other people from my past and my family were in the building. I opened a door and looked into a dark room. Daren was there on the floor lying in a sleeping bag. Without a word he opened the side of the sleeping bag so I could crawl in next to him. I did. He took me into his embrace, our bodies softly melting into one another. Then, just as we were about to kiss, the door opened and the light turned on. Someone interrupted us. I had no choice but to go. Had I been able to stay, I knew a state of total completion and union lay before me. A feeling of deep satisfaction and contentment. Instead, I was left alone with myself, feeling bereft and incomplete.

Steve's interpretation, along the lines of Jung, was that Daren represented the male part of me I was trying to connect with. This internal union would create the completion I was looking for. It's the same interpretation I would have said to anyone asking my advice, but I wanted a more romantic interpretation.

Part of me still believed in the well-worn fairytale of my youth, and this dream could be made to fit that epic tale. Princess separated from her Prince by a series of events that take them on grand and treacherous adventures spanning continents. Through an unexpected series of events they meet, but the Princess has already been promised to someone else whom she loves. Years later she is free and begins to dream once again of her Prince. But even in her dreams she cannot be with him. Just as in her youth, fate constantly intervenes keeping the Prince eternally out of her reach. Both exist just a hair's breadth away from complete union. Both believe the other can fulfill their longing for completion.

This was the version I was voting for. Much more engaging, I thought. Of course I did not divulge my fantasy interpretation to Steve. I did however re-word it to sound more "adult" before I bounced it off of him.

"You don't think it means that there is something incomplete that needs to be finished? You don't think it has anything to do with Daren at all?"

I was hoping Steve would give me some room here to keep my dream. He, however, did not get the telegram.

"No, I don't think it has anything to do with him. This has to do with something in yourself that feels incomplete. He reflects that to you, but it is not about him."

I let the subject drop. I suppose I knew he was right, but I didn't want to listen. I was single, Steve had a girlfriend, and though my journey with him had brought me to the brink of self-empowerment, the sense of union hinted at in my dream beckoned. Part of me was still convinced the only way to get there from here was through a man.

This time, I told myself, I just need to make sure I have the sex and the passion. Then it will work.

CHAPTER EIGHTEEN

Weeks and months passed. My dreams became more consistent and more real. Every time I would wake up with an intense feeling of longing. In passing, I mentioned it to Steve again.

"Why don't you call him?" he said. "Tell him how you feel."

"I can't do that!" I exclaimed. "And anyway, even if I did call him, there is no way I could reach him. He always has women around him."

"Okay, then don't," he replied. Men. So cut and dried. I was expecting him to push or encourage me a little more like girlfriends do with each other, but no. He did have a point. Either I was going to do it or not. If I wasn't ready, there was no point in talking about it.

I thought about Steve's suggestion for a long time. One afternoon I was lying in bed having a nap. I suddenly woke with absolute clarity and lack of fear. I knew it was time to find Daren and tell him how I felt.

My intent was not necessarily to be in a relationship with Daren, but to complete the past. I needed to put away my fairytale for good so I could move on with my life. It might mean we would end up in a relationship, but more likely it would mean we would both acknowledge our collective past and bury it. I felt I needed to do this. If I did not, my dream of what could be with Daren would thwart the possibility of future relationships.

I got up out of bed, rifling through my agenda to find the last number I had for him. It was the number of a yoga center he had started with his sister. I dialed the number, my body tense with anticipation. Now that the decision had been made, I could feel the pressure building. It would not let off until I had said what I needed to say and had my final answer. The phone rang once, twice, three times. Nothing. No answer. Just as I was about to hang up, a female voice picked up. She was breathless, having apparently run for the phone.

"Liz?" I said. "Is that you?"

"Yes," she replied inquiringly. "Who's this?"

"Hi! This is Kamini! It's been such a long time since I've heard your voice. How are you?"

I had reached Daren's sister, Liz. As we chatted, I could feel the pressure building. It was almost unbearable. When would I be able to ask the question I so wanted to ask without being rude? Finally, I could no longer hold it back. The words jumped out of my mouth before I could stop them.

"I'm actually calling for Daren. Is he around by any chance? Could I speak with him?" I said, trying not to appear too eager.

Daren had given me his card with these coordinates a couple of years before when we had last seen each other. I had not called or made contact since then. It was my one and only link to him. Now I was counting on it. My heart sank with her next words.

"Actually, he's not here. I haven't heard from him in a long time."

Daren had left the yoga center. In fact, without warning he had left teaching altogether, and had taken off to his land in British Columbia where no one could reach him. He was off the grid and unreachable by phone, fax or email. No one had heard from him in months.

"But," she went on, "I was walking down Young Street today and happened to run into a friend of mine, who happened to talk to a friend of hers today on Victoria Island."

Liz was in Toronto, on the east coast of Canada. Victoria Island was a good 3,000 miles away off the west coast, just above Washington State. I listened politely as she continued, my hopes of any kind of reunion with Daren sinking fast.

"She said her friend recognized Daren walking down the street. She approached him to say hello, and he mentioned he would be staying for one night in Victoria with a couple by the name of Bob and Ruth."

That was not a lot of information. It would be impossible for me to find Daren with that little. Thanking Liz for her help, I hung up. I was finally ready to declare my love and the recipient of my heartfelt declaration was MIA! Oh, well I told myself. I tried. It must be the way it is supposed to be. Let it go and move on. But something inside me would not let go. It was time. I knew it was time. No matter that reality wasn't making it easy. I still knew, to the core of my being, the moment was now. I would not give up without a fight. I began to turn over the conversation with Liz in my head.

"Bob and Ruth on Victoria," I thought. "Bob and Ruth. Bob and Ruth." Why did those names sound familiar? Did they? Or did I just want them to sound familiar? Had I known a Canadian couple named Bob and Ruth as a child at the yoga center? Hmmm. I wasn't sure, but I knew someone who might be.

From my little apartment in Holland, I called my brother in Pennsylvania. On the first ring he answered. Luckily, my brother and I have one of those relationships that don't require small talk, so I jumped right in.

"Can you look up something on your database for me?" I asked with an equal measure of desperation and urgency. He got the message. This was important to me. I could almost feel him sit up to attention.

"Sure. What do you need?"

"Can you see if there is anyone with the first names of Bob and Ruth in the database on Victoria Island, Canada?"

I knew it was a longshot. I had no last name, and my brother would have to search everyone on Victoria by hand. But it was all I had and I was taking it. If I wasn't going to get my happy ending, I was surely going to make sure I had done everything I could before I gave up.

I listened intently, trying to make meaning out of the silence broken only by the subtle strains of keys clicking through the transatlantic phone line. The answer to come would determine my future one way or the other. I had no choice but to see what the universe would bring. Would it be time for us? Would I find Daren? Or would it yet again be a near miss—just as so many of the dreams I had had before? After what seemed like an eternity, but in truth less than a minute, my brother's voice came back on the line.

"Yes, I do have a Bob and Ruth White on Victoria Island. Is that who you are looking for?"

I couldn't believe it! Maybe this was it? Hastily I grabbed a pen and wrote down the phone number he had for them. I quickly thanked him and hung up. Nothing was certain yet. There were a thousand things that could go wrong. I was in Holland; Daren was in Victoria, thousands of miles away. I had the name of a Bob and Ruth, but was it the right Bob and Ruth? Was Daren even there? If he was only staying for one night, he might have already gone. I had only the most tenuous of threads tying me to a possible future with him, and I was about to find out if that thread would prove to break or not.

Telephone number in hand, I dialed Canada. God only knew what my phone bill was going to look like, but I didn't care one whit. This was my life we were talking about, and I was about to take the biggest gamble yet.

The phone rang and someone picked up. I held my breath until the disembodied voice on the other end repeated that automated sentence I had heard so many times before, "The number you have reached is no longer in service. Please check the number and dial again." And dial again I did. Again, it did not go through.

I felt I was standing on the edge of a cliff, ready to jump. I did not know the outcome of the jump. I might fly, or I might sink like a stone. But the outcome was irrelevant. Something beyond my brain and my intellect was propelling me over that cliff, yet just as I thought I was going to be able to finally do it, an invisible net kept stopping me. Was this a sign? Was I supposed to give up? Or was it a sign that I should keep going? I didn't care. I was going.

Now armed with a surname, I called Canadian information, praying the Bob and Ruth my brother had told me about were still in Victoria and listed in the phone book. If not, it would be a dead end. By the time I found them, the small window of time I had to find Daren with this couple, if they *were* the right couple, would pass.

By now, my nerves were beginning to settle a little bit. I was coming close to the end, whatever it would be. And as I did, I found myself becoming more and more calm and peaceful. One way or another, the situation would resolve itself. I would know what the next step in my life would look like.

As providence would have it, Bob and Ruth White *were* listed in the Victoria phone book under a new number. I held the line and wrote it down. I called, and could hear the phone ringing on the other end.

Very soon now. The phone picked up and a woman with an English accent came on the line. Instantly, I recognized that voice.

"Ruth?" I said. "This is Kamini. Do you remember me?"

It turned out I had known Ruth, and why her name sounded so familiar to me. Way back when I was 16 years old and participated in that first dance training Daren was supposed to lead, she was there. Ruth had been one of the participants in the training with me. That was how she had known Daren, and me as well. Small world.

"Kamini! Oh, my God. I can't believe it! Do you know who's here?"

"I'm hoping I know who's there. That's why I'm calling."

All these years, my connection with Daren had been repeatedly thwarted. It was never right, never time; something always came in between to stop us. Just like my dreams. But in this moment, something happened. I felt as if the heavens parted and a channel opened up as clearly as if I had said "Open Sesame," and all the riches that had been withheld were suddenly available to me.

"Hold on," she said. "He's right here." I could hear muffled voices and exclamations in the background and some shuffling as a certain someone else came to the phone. My heart was racing, my shoulders tense with anticipation as I listened.

Suddenly I heard that deep, familiar voice, and I felt a stirring all the way up my spine. My soul knew that voice.

"Kamini?!" he said in absolute shock and stunned surprise. "How on earth did you find me? No one, absolutely no one, knows I'm here."

Daren had been living on his land deep in the interior of British Columbia without electricity, running water, or a phone. Out of the blue, he had decided to go to Victoria. As he was walking down the street there, he noticed a health food store and stopped in to buy a few items for lunch. Waiting near the cash register to pay he noticed a flyer for yoga classes taught by Ruth White. Recognizing her as a former student, he took one of her cards posted underneath and gave her a call. In the course of their conversation Ruth invited him to stay overnight. He accepted, for one night, before beginning the 14-hour drive home the next morning. It was the only night he was available by telephone. I had found him on that one night. He had not expected to hear from anyone since it was only by sheer coincidence he was there in the first place. And here I was calling him from across the ocean!

"Well, I just wanted to tell you two things. One, I'm divorced. Two, I have no attachment to the outcome on this, but I just need to say that my feelings for you are still there. I just need to say it to complete, acknowledge it, and let go. You don't have to do anything or say anything. I just need you to know it. That's all."

I waited as he absorbed this statement. He chuckled as if enjoying his own private thoughts. I waited.

"Get on a plane and come over," he said with assured urgency. "It is our time."

CHAPTER NINETEEN

I couldn't quite fathom what I was hearing. I couldn't believe I was hearing those words in real life. I had heard them so often in my head, but now it was real. In an instant I snapped to life. We made plans to meet up in less than two weeks. Bob and Ruth offered to host us. Daren said his land would be inhospitable at that time of year and I left it at that.

He would go home and then come back to meet me on Victoria Island. I frantically packed my bags, purchased tickets and re-arranged my work schedule. My friends, who'd not really heard much about Daren up until this time were subjected to several rounds of Daren stories.

Finally the day came. My bags were carefully packed. I would have lots of time to reflect on how our first meeting would go. My first flight, to New York City, was about eight hours. Then another six to Seattle. From Seattle to Vancouver, and then a small charter flight from Vancouver to Victoria. To this day I cannot recall any details of the flights. I was so focused and willing to do anything to get there, I would have traveled twice the distance.

As we landed in Victoria, I was at the back of the plane. I was the last to emerge and walked down the flight stairs and across the tarmac to the small flight building in the distance. I imagined Daren's eyes following me across the tarmac as I walked. I stood a little straighter, tummy in, chest out. No harm in trying to put my best qualities forward! I could not see him, but he could probably see me. It had been years since we had seen each other in person. I didn't know if the chemistry would still be there or what he would look like.

As I walked through the double doors, I paused. A circle of people had gathered around to greet arriving passengers. My eyes scanned left and right. Then, as if appearing from nowhere, Daren stepped through the center of the crowd. He looked straight into my eyes, opened his arms and held me closely to him as if he would never let go. We kissed. For once, I was not shy or self-conscious. This was our moment. I couldn't believe after all these years I was finally free to engage in such a simple act without any repercussions.

As we stepped back slightly and moved away from the group he said, "I have never seen you look more beautiful." I loved him for that. In my mind it was a bald-faced lie since he had known me in the blush of my youth and beauty. But I loved him for it nonetheless since I wanted to be as beautiful as I could be in his eyes. We took hands and walked towards Bob and Ruth who were waiting discreetly off to one side. We greeted one another and made our way to their home.

That night we made love for the first time. True to form, Bob and Ruth had put us in separate rooms. Daren was sleeping in the yoga room only accessible from the outside. I waited for silence to fall in the household before I crept downstairs. Daren was waiting for me. One candle lit. The house was on stilts, high up in the trees. We were surrounded by windows. The air was chilly. Daren lifted his blanket and I slid into bed next to him. After years of imagining this instant, our bodies were flesh to flesh. But unlike my dreams, no one interrupted us. No one would stop us. As Daren gathered me into his embrace, I turned my cheek to rest on his chest. I felt his heartbeat. Our hands found each other's bodies.

Our lovemaking was unlike anything I had experienced before. All those years I had so dearly loved my Steve, I'd always felt I had missed out on a full expression of the physical side of love. Now I had finally experienced the part I thought I was missing.

Our days together followed like a dream. We couldn't get enough of holding, touching, kissing, laughing, talking. The floodgates had opened up. In actual fact, we'd never really had time to truly talk to one another or get to know each other on a deeper level because of the various limiting factors dating back from the first time we'd met. My idea of Daren was based on short snippets of conversation snatched in small private moments. The rest had been filled out by my imagination.

We made plans to meet up again. Daren would come to meet me in Holland in a few months time. I went home in a daze. My friends, my work, were all there to greet me. I was happy to be home.

At night, when my work was done I would often light a candle and sit alone looking at pictures we had taken during our week in Victoria. Something new had begun, and it was anyone's guess if it would go anywhere. But I would nurture the moments we had had together. No one could take that from me.

Soon, days became weeks and then months. I began to prepare my apartment for Daren to arrive, cleaning everything from top to bottom, buying new sheets, some new clothes, and taking in some extra yoga classes in the hopes of maximizing my chances of looking aesthetically pleasing in the buff. The closer the day came, the more I fantasized how it would be. This visit to Amsterdam would be completely different from the last one.

The morning of Daren's arrival, I got up early, carefully preparing the apartment with flowers, a bowl of fruit, a bottle of champagne, some chocolate. I went to the train station and purchased two tickets—a round-trip for me and a one-way for him from the airport to the Central Station of Amsterdam. I still couldn't believe he was coming.

Arriving at the airport, I checked his flight information and made my way to the arrival gate. Now the shoe was on the other foot. I was among the group of greeters waiting for their loved ones. My excitement was high. My cheeks flushed, a smile on my face I simply could not erase. He would be here any moment now. Person after person in singles, pairs and triads exited those doors. As many of them stepped beyond the gates, family members, friends, or loved ones would greet them. I watched them all and waited. I went to check that I was at the right arrival gate. Yes. I asked some of those exiting if they had been on the flight from Canada. Yes.

By now it had been over an hour. Had something happened? Had he been delayed by customs? Had his baggage been lost? I waited another hour. My excitement had long since been replaced by worry. What had happened? A guard came by to close this particular exit. I approached him, holding back my tears as I explained to him what had happened and whom I was waiting for. Taking pity on me, he asked me to wait while he called customs to see if anyone from the flight had been detained. Nothing. Their records showed that everyone from the flight had deplaned with no problems. I couldn't believe it. How could this be? Had he changed his mind? Why had I not heard anything? My mind was racing. I began to walk slowly back towards the train, my mind frozen in disbelief. I had no idea what to feel.

I didn't bother to take a seat in the train. I didn't want others to see me. I could feel the tears building behind my eyes. I just wanted to lick my wounds in private. What I hadn't seen was a beautiful, almost angelic looking blonde woman sitting on the stairs just around the corner from me. But she had seen me.

"You seem like you are in so much pain," she said, breaking the silence. "What happened?"

I didn't want to go into the whole story so I simply said, "My boyfriend, who was supposed to be at the airport, didn't come."

She looked at me empathetically but with absolute, almost mystical certainty, "You have all the love you need within you, you just haven't recognized it. That is why you are in pain."

The power in her words momentarily broke through the haze of my inner drama. I knew there was something significant and powerful in those words that I not only needed to hear, but needed to truly understand. That was my moment, my chance to get it. But I was not ready. I was convinced Daren was my ticket to happiness. I would have to go for many more years before I realized through my own experience the profound truth the woman on the train spoke to me that day.

I waited for two days, hearing nothing. I didn't want to believe Daren would drop me in that way. Something must have happened.

Then I received a call from a friend whose apartment I had been renting for a couple of months before moving to this one. He'd gotten a call for me from a "Daren," who had misplaced my new number and only had this old one. He'd ridden a bus for 18 hours to Calgary and waited all day to get on the plane. Just as he was checking in he was refused. His passport had expired. He'd had to turn around and take that same bus 18 hours back home. He could not call me because he'd lost my number. Luckily, my friend had my new phone number and had given it to Daren. He would be calling the next time he was in a town with a pay phone. Of course there was no phone on his land. All I could do was wait.

Steve, hearing of some of the details of this latest event through mutual friends, called me. "If he's this unprepared now, he's not going to be able to take care of you."

I refused to listen to Steve's urgings, convinced such a mistake could happen to anyone. In the face of my stubborn refusal to listen, Steve gave way. He had no say in it anyway.

A few days later, with Steve's admonition to break it off with Daren still ringing in my ears, I got a call. It was Daren. He would not be able to secure a passport for several months. He suggested I come to visit him. All caution thrown to the wind, I agreed immediately. This was Daren we were talking about. Caution did not count. In this case I would throw myself into it fully and take whatever came. This was one time I would not look back with thoughts of what could have been.

As I went over to Steve's to arrange some of my affairs, I told him my plans. I could tell he didn't agree, but he only said, "One thing I respect about you is whatever you do, you do it completely. You are one person who will never look back on your life and wish you had taken more chances, because you take them all."

Within a few days I was on a plane to Calgary, which was still about eight hours by car from Daren's land. Daren no longer had a car and did not know how he was going to come get me, but he said he'd find a way. Stepping out of customs I did not know if he would be there, especially given our most recent fiasco. But he was. His son had agreed to make the drive with his girlfriend and their young daughter. We cuddled together in the back against the cold as we made the long trip back home.

The following morning we arrived at Daren's land. As we had been coming closer, I could feel Daren becoming more and more excited. The scenery was stunningly beautiful and became increasingly more mountainous as we approached his home. I knew Daren lived close to the land. I told myself I could live simply. No problem. I could do anything for my guy.

Finally, our long journey ended as we pulled off the road and into a makeshift driveway. I got out of the car and stepped onto the rocky exposed soil, trying not to twist my ankle in my high-heeled, citified version of country boots. In front of us was an army green tent structure and what looked like a partially-covered outdoor kitchen area. To my right was a trailer. I could already tell the cute outfits I had carefully chosen for this trip would be woefully inappropriate. I would be a fish out of water here. In the far distance beyond the land I could see the stunning glacial blue waters of a lake backed by white-topped mountains. It was spring. The air was slightly chilly, but I was still comfortable. I wasn't sure where we would be staying. I stood uncertainly as Daren's son pulled out of the driveway. Would it be the tent or the trailer?

Daren took my bags and strode towards the trailer. Previously, he told me cheerfully, he'd lived in a teepee. The trailer was a luxury addition to the land. Relieved, I followed him inside. I had never even been camping. Coming from the city to a place with no electricity or running water would be challenging enough. The idea of having a conventional roof over our heads was comforting to me.

Inside Daren had made his home cozy and welcoming. The far end of the trailer consisted of cathedral windows looking out onto the lake and the mountains behind. Just in front of the windows, lay a bed on the floor, invitingly arranged with fresh sheets and a fluffy duvet. This, I would be comfortable with.

Daren continued with a tour of the house, showing me how he used water hauled from the river to wash dishes in a basin, the water heated over a wood stove. Then he gave me the bathroom lesson. I had two choices. I could go outside and crouch over the hole 30 yards or so past the end of the trailer (and in full view of the bed), or I could line the toilet in the trailer with a plastic bag, go in there and then dispose of the bag and its contents in the appointed receptacle outdoors. My body more or less chose option number three–not going to the bathroom at all.

I could feel my trepidation about being here in an unfamiliar environment begin to take root. But I deliberately ignored the feeling. Not even the Canadian wilderness was going to get in the way of my dream. I was going to make it happen no matter what. After all, destiny had brought us together hadn't it? That meant it would all work out.

That night was magic, a thousand stars filling a boundless, inky sky. No sign of human existence marring the intense beauty, the sounds of nature; the moon creating a silvery reflection off the lake in the far distance. It was indeed a special place here. Through my discomfort, I could see why Daren had chosen to retreat here.

The next morning, I awoke to a rumbling stomach. There was a refrigerator, but of course without electricity it didn't work. It suddenly occurred to me we had no car. How were we going to get out? How did we get water to drink? Was I supposed to drink the water from the river? The answer turned out to be,

"Yes, just avoid drinking the flecks of silt." All the things I usually took for granted were no longer obvious to me.

Daren heartily announced we had bikes and would cycle to breakfast. In my mind I thought breakfast couldn't be more than a few miles away, and living in Holland I was a good biker. It wasn't until we got back out onto the road that I remembered where we were. The terrain in this part of Canada is not hilly; it is mountainous. In fact, professionals from all over the world come to train here for competitions such as the Tour de France. I was used to flat terrain with a few hills here and there. This was like nothing I'd ever seen, but I was determined nothing would get between me and what I wanted, so off we went.

Three hours and twenty-two kilometers later, we arrived at our breakfast venue. I'd had no water, my skin crusty with sweat, my legs trembling with fatigue. It was already lunchtime. As I got off my bike I told myself to straighten up, trying not to look as broken as I felt. Our meal was a welcome respite.

After about an hour, we walked back towards our bikes. I had no idea how I could make it another 22 kilometers over those mountains back to the land. Biking up the last long hill, I ordered my legs to work. They valiantly struggled to make it to the top. It took every ounce of strength I had. In the same way I had willed this dream of Daren into existence, I was now using everything I had to get me to a place where I could let go and allow gravity to take me home.

Ahead, at the top of the hill, Daren had pulled out into a lookout point. He watched as I covered the last bit of distance between us, my legs screaming, my face red with heat–a picture of total and complete exhaustion. I was almost there. Then I pulled up next to him and got off the bike. We walked hand-in-hand to the edge of the cliff overlooking a valley dotted with farmhouses, lakes and intermittent stretches of uncultivated land.

Looking out into the distance, Daren said aloud, "We've made it to the top. It's all downhill from here."

We both knew he wasn't just talking about biking. It had been so many years of resigning ourselves to the idea there would never be a time for us. Now, seemingly against all odds, we had made it to the top of the mountain. Our fairytale had come true. Like the top of this hill, how could it not be easy going from now on? Hadn't we already done the hard work? Now we were together, the rest would be easy. Or so I believed.

CHAPTER TWENTY

S HORTLY AFTER THAT TRIP to Canada I lost the sublet to my apartment in Amsterdam, and decided to move to British Columbia. I began packing my things, putting my larger items in storage and sending a few boxes by mail. The more real my move became the stronger my doubts took hold. An inner voice was telling me very strongly I was about to jump from the frying pan into the fire. If I thought being with Steve was challenging, it was a piece of cake compared to what I would be facing in the wilderness, with no phone, no car, no electricity, no running water—not to mention being in a new relationship. Part of me, the part I tried desperately to ignore, knew I had a nearly impossible task ahead of me. But I had to do it anyway. If not, I would always be thinking I had missed out on the great love of my life. I had to find out for myself. I had to take a chance.

I flew from Amsterdam to Calgary again. This time Daren would be working and would not be able to pick me up. I arrived on my own with two suitcases. I then boarded a bus and had the next 18 hours to wonder about my new life, and how it would look. I was excited and terrified at the same time.

Arriving exhausted but eager, Daren picked me up at the bus stop, and a friend of his drove us to the land. This time, as we walked into the trailer, I looked through different eyes. This was my home now. There was no going back.

The first night, Daren looked at me seriously and asked, "Are you sure you want to do this?"

"Yes," I replied, perhaps with a bit more confidence than I really felt. "Are you?"

He paused for several seconds before replying, "I'm afraid I will hurt you. I hurt my ex-wife, and I don't want to do that to you," he said, uncertainly.

"I'm a big girl," I replied. "It is not your job to keep me from getting hurt. This is what I want. I'm willing to take the consequences."

Slowly, he nodded his head, coming over to me and putting his head on my shoulder. I held him.

In the days to come, however, I found myself in a state of withdrawal. The trailer, being not completely airtight, had various animals living with us. Insects from outside, mice in the kitchen. There was really nothing we could do about it. At night, we would try to protect the food we had as best as we could. In the morning we never knew what we would still be able to eat. Perishables we kept in an icebox, with ice purchased from the store. But the ice would inevitably melt before we could get more, and if not properly put into airtight containers, our food would be soaking in water.

I took my solace in the one place I felt comfortable, the bed. I would find myself running off to the "bathroom" or kitchen, and then running back to the bed as if it was home base. The one place I felt safe. But even that was not a safe haven.

One morning, after a very good night's sleep, I awoke with the sun on my face and Daren next to me. We had had a wonderful night and I was feeling better that morning. With a smile on my face I stretched my arms, awakening my body from its sleep, my hands naturally dropping onto the outside of the blanket. But instead of finding blanket, my hands found something else. Something warm, sticky and a little mushy. My brain would not compute. What was this? I lifted up my hand to see it covered with blood. I looked down to see a partially decapitated and gutted baby rabbit. I started to scream. I have never seen Daren move so fast as he scooped up the entire blanket and carried my little "gift" from the cat outdoors.

Daren, doing his best to give me time to adjust, would prepare our meals on the woodstove—or with the propane oven if we had propane. I would sit on the bed and watch him start the fire. Once, while he was out working, I tried to help by starting the woodstove on my own. I failed miserably.

From Fantasy to Reality

I found myself crying every day without fail. Never having camped a day in my life, I had no context for living without the comforts I was used to. The contrast between my city life in Amsterdam with my cute clothes, my lunches with friends and the luxuries of transportation, food, and water was a far cry from this. And there was more.

We didn't have a car. The nearest small town was about 14 kilometers away. If we wanted to get anywhere without biking, or if we needed to buy groceries or do laundry, we had no other choice but to hitchhike.

In this part of Canada, hitchhiking was very common-place. No one thought anything of it, and it was generally safe. But like the rest of my generation, I had been filled with horror stories about hitchhiking and how I should never ever do it under any circumstances. So, it stood to reason that, even with Daren, the prospect of hitchhiking was terrifying. Every time I got into a car, I was waiting to be chopped up into little pieces. But the alternative, walking or biking would be nearly impossible. I would often find myself chanting as we were standing on the side of the road, "Please give me a ride. Please don't kill me. Please give me a ride. Please don't kill me."

As all this was happening, I watched my savings quickly dwindling. Daren and I would have work in the spring and summer, but until then we supplemented with my savings and eventually my credit cards. Watching my debt mount I grew more and more afraid. I had always paid my debts on time. I had always been a model citizen. Now our current debts, plus debts Daren had incurred before my arrival were pressing on me. Being the "good girl," I felt I had to take responsibility for all of this.

Though we always managed to have food of some kind, it was not always ideal or enough for the two of us, plus Daren's son and granddaughter. I had never in my entire life been in a situation where food was in question, even to the slightest degree. To have something so basic put into question touched one of my most primitive fears.

To say I was on my edge in practically every way imaginable would have been an understatement. I realized we all have basic survival needs, like food and shelter. Those real needs are actually very minimal. But layered on top of those true physical needs for survival are our psychological needs for survival. This is what I was coming up against. Though I rationally knew my physical body was not in jeopardy, my mental and emotional concept of what I thought I needed to survive was very much threatened. It pushed me in to a constant level of stress as if I were truly fighting to live. Though I was nowhere near homeless, I do feel I had the smallest of glimpses into what it is like.

To this day if a destitute person asks me for money, I will rarely say no. And I always treat the person I'm speaking to with respect. There are so many people who went out of their way to help us in so many little miraculous ways, I can't help but pass it on.

The interesting thing is that among those who have to struggle to survive, there is a code of mutual help and giving. Everyone brings what they have to share. If one person has a car and another has a couple of dollars, they will team up so both can drive. If one person gets a short-term construction job, they will try to get a job for their friend as well. Or one will lend the other their tools, so at least one of them can work. When people come to dinner, they will bring anything they have—whether it is carrots from the garden or Rice Krispies—always to be given and received with gratitude and dignity.

Despite the bits of help from many unexpected avenues, I found I couldn't get out of living in a constant state of defensiveness; trying to protect myself from what felt like an alien world around me. Somehow, my instinct to survive had overshadowed my easygoing, happy-go-lucky self. In her place was a surly, sulky girl who could not relax with the ever-changing geography of her new life. I had lost my footing and could not find a way back to myself except in small glimpses. Instead, I was stuck with a part of me I had never known existed.

In an attempt to make myself easier to live with, I put on a happy face. I tried to be the person I used to be. But the slightest incident would cause that mask to drop. I had myself tied up in knots trying be someone different than the tightly wound person I had become. Though Daren had some idea of how I felt, I didn't feel I could share my difficulties with him. This was the life he loved and wanted. In not loving this life, I was not loving him. It was a very sensitive and personal subject.

Often, Daren's son and granddaughter would be with us as well. Since Daren was my sole reason for being here, I relied on having time just for the two of us. When we did have that time, it went a long way to easing my inner pain. Some nights, hitch-hiking back from the nearest city, about an hour away by car, we'd have enough resources to pick up a bottle of wine. Daren would make us a lovely meal. Sometimes we'd have batteries in the CD player and we would do partner yoga, dance around the cabin together, give each other massages and make love by the warmth of the woodstove and candlelight. Then Daren would make us pancakes for dessert. It was truly special and magical. Those were the moments that kept me going.

But, as is the case with any family, the presence of others was too often an easy excuse for us not to talk about the issues we were facing or take the time we needed for each other. My desire for closeness, combined with my inability to make it happen without appearing completely selfish, only caused me to retreat deeper into my own world.

Usually, I have other people to talk to and help me move through something like this. But I had no phone, no computer or email, and no one to even talk to unless I could find a way to the neighboring town. Even then, I was reluctant to tell anyone just how difficult it was for me. I didn't want to worry my parents. And I certainly didn't want to admit that, not only had my fairytale not panned out according to plan, I felt isolated and very much alone.

Still I would not give up. I was convinced destiny had brought us together. That meant we were *supposed* to be together. We were supposed to have our happy ending. If I just hung on a little longer, I could make it happen.

Not only that, but I had essentially invested my life in this dream coming true from the time I was sixteen. If I admitted my fairytale was a bust, I would be saying one of the foundations upon which my life was based was false. It would mean I had been wasting all this time, emotion and energy on a fool's journey. Of course there was also the fact that I had already ended one major relationship. That was bad enough. I couldn't call it quits now. That would mean I was not able to follow through on relationships.

HANGING ON

Once we decide on a picture of happiness and the person who will fulfill it, we invest the major portion of our life energy in it. When it seems that the picture may not yield desired results, we try harder, we hold on longer. We dig our heels in and insist to ourselves that just around the corner is the absolution we are looking for; the reward that will make all the hardship and sacrifice worthwhile. Sometimes that reward comes, and we are well satisfied. But often, it doesn't. And we are left with a choice: do we keep going? Or do we cut our losses and move on? Many of us keep going because to admit we were wrong would be to admit all the time, resources and energy we put into it was for naught. Though that is not really the case, few of us are ready to do that. Instead, we may keep going, waiting for the day when things will change and we will be compensated for having borne so much for so long.

But it's not a life rule that by submitting to what we don't like, we'll get what we like. Life doesn't work that way. It will not suddenly change its form to fit our wants just because we've put in time. Yet this was a subtle underlying assumption I was operating from.

As spring and summer came, Daren and I worked at a spa about an hour and a half away in another valley. We would both make some money from which we could live for a time. During those times, I could relax. We stayed at the spa. We had beds, a toilet and got fed every day. Not surprisingly, it was also the time Daren and I would get along the best.

Having that little bit of space from the intensity of my life, I began to see it was up to me to make the best of what I had. I could continue to play the victim to my circumstance, I could put in time in the hopes that life would bring me something more desirable, or I could take some steps to create a life I could live. I had to at least try to take charge of my own life. Then we would see what happened from there. My father used to say, "Your life is not in what comes to you, but how you are with what comes to you." This was my moment to step up and try to be with the life I had in a different way.

ADJUSTING TO MEET REALITY

Over time, I metaphorically began to venture from the safety of my bed. I began to branch out and do the things that felt right for me. Instead of allowing myself to collapse under the weight of such a different lifestyle, I started to push back. I learned how to start a fire, to chop wood, and heat water to wash dishes. I fixed doors that wouldn't close, patched holes in the roof and in walls where animals were coming into the house.

Though we'd had a truck for a while, it was so unreliable, we still found ourselves piling out of it on a regular basis and hitchhiking the rest of the way to where we were going. Finally, the truck found its final resting place at a garage where it was deemed too expensive to fix.

I saved up all my money to buy a car. I purchased an old Honda for $1200. I worked hard to make that money, giving five to six massages a day at times, in addition to accompanying the guests on daily hikes of 12-15 kilometers through the mountains. I have never been so excited or proud of having bought anything in my life. It was my ticket to greater freedom.

Daren used money he'd made for us to build a simple cabin in the woods down by the river that ran through our property. Neither of us had any experience with building, and we couldn't afford a contractor, but we came up with a clever idea. A friend of ours had had a beautiful cedar shed made. What if this person could build us a cedar shed, but longer, with nice windows, insulated, and with a chimney for a wood stove? Taken with the idea, we went to meet the shed builder. He'd never done anything like it, but said he'd give it a try. He'd even be able to add a deck to the front and the side. The side deck would serve as an outdoor kitchen as there would not be enough room inside. Wiring and plumbing was not an issue, so it seemed doable. Excited, we went to a store that sold used windows and sliding doors, planning where everything would go.

In the meantime, I had accepted a job offer from my dad. My father needed teachers to staff his yoga teacher training, and I was offered a position. I readily agreed. It would mean two trips of 10 days to the U.S., but I would be paid, and that would mean more money for both of us. It would also give me a chance to get off the land and back away from my edge a little, enough to get some breathing space and come back to myself a little bit.

I also persuaded Daren as the founder of a unique style of yoga, to offer a training of his own. I promised I would assist him and do all the marketing and registrations. I rented a space in a small storeroom of a closed store in a nearby town. I could get a phone and internet service there. That little storeroom became my safe haven. It was freezing cold in the winter, but it was my space. I had a toilet that flushed. I had a sink. I had a phone. I had a computer. I put out all my files. I set up a little space amidst what felt like the disorder of the rest of my life. I had my own telephone number where my parents could reach me. I had a line to the outside world.

CHAPTER TWENTY-ONE

THOUGH I NOW had my office in place, it was soon clear that all the basic necessities of life such as food, water, dishes, laundry, and transport were still taking the major portion of our energy. To manage this, I had taken to carrying around a backpack. In it I had all my pending office work—my agenda, my call list and to do list.

Any time we made it off the land I would hasten myself to the closest available pay phone or public computer to attend to these things. I also made sure I always had my toiletry bag and a towel along in case we came upon someone we knew who would let me use their shower. Running water was a luxury.

With any remaining time, I would go to my little office. Daren would often drop me off and then pick me up. I diligently worked on a manual for my dad's yoga teacher training. Then on one for Daren's partner yoga training. With Daren's friend Wendy, we updated his website, rented a location and posted information on an upcoming training with Daren. I took the phone calls and inquiries in my office. I felt I had taken control of my life and had carved out a space where I could be me. Though my life here was still not ideal in many ways, I felt that I had made it the best it could be under the circumstances.

LIFE'S PLAN DOESN'T ALWAYS FIT OUR PLAN

The hardest part for me was letting go of control—the need to get things done or to get somewhere. One time, when we were hitchhiking again for one reason or another, I expressed this frustration to Daren. I told him I couldn't get anywhere. Every time I tried to take a step forward it felt like I was taking three, or even four, steps back. We could spend an entire day (and we often did) just trying to get from the land to town to clean up, do laundry and the like. We could easily spend three hours waiting for a ride on the side of the road.

With almost the whole of our lives taken up in attending to the most basic things, I could not fulfill my own drive to succeed or get ahead. Every time I fixed one thing, something else would fall apart. For once in my life I could not keep it all together, and it was driving me crazy.

"Where are you trying to get?" Daren asked, after letting me vent for a few minutes.

That shut me up. And it was a very good question. Where *was* I trying to get? A place where nothing would ever fall apart again? Logically that would never happen, yet that was exactly what I was trying to do. I had a picture in my head of a perfect life where all the problems that plagued us now would be solved and no new ones could appear. Then my life would resemble the picture of what I thought it should be, we would be happy and I would finally be able to relax from my constant struggle to get life to be something different than what it was. But the reality was that this *was* my reality. Things would always be falling out of place while other things were falling into place.

I would soon come to realize life is in a constant ebb and flow and will rarely meet all our needs at any one given time. That isn't because life is against us. It is because that is not the nature of life. Life's nature is to flow. It will never get to a place where everything is permanently, exactly the way we want it.

Though I never let go of my need to get somewhere completely, I began to see the driving need I had to get somewhere in order to be happy, was in part the cause of my unhappiness. If I could relax my death grip on life, maybe I could give space for it to be as it was. I could be more relaxed with things falling into and out of place all the time. It didn't mean I would renounce my goals and desire to succeed. But it did mean I could be a little happier and more relaxed along the way, even when life was not falling into place according to my plans.

I still continued to pursue the aspects of my life that enlivened me. I got more work in the U.S. and would fly down once every three months or so. It was a 4½ hour drive over the border just to get to the airport.

During that time I began to discover myself as a teacher in a way I had not known. I found myself leading larger and larger crowds, not just in association with my father, but also in my own right. I was coming into my own as a teacher and though I had taught for years before, I was discovering it as a vehicle through which I could bring my self-expression into the world.

A NEW HOME

After one of these trips I came home to our new cabin. Our shed builder had teamed up with Daren and had put our new home into place. Daren had already painstakingly moved many of our things down below. The house could not be easily accessed by car or truck so most things had to be walked down the steep grade on foot. Our new home appealed to my aesthetic sensibilities. The cedar shingled dwelling radiated a homey charm. It would be our place to retreat from everything else. A shielded patio covered the entrance, giving us shelter and a place to put our muddy boots and assorted items.

The side deck directly overlooked a ravine, at the bottom of which ran a fast-flowing river. Tree branches hung over the river as it thundered around mossy rocks and fallen trees to a lake just out of sight. Ferns grew tall and mighty in the mist of the river. It was truly an awe-inspiring sight.

Friends and family gifted us with the means to buy furniture, a propane stove, heater and refrigerator. The side deck was partially covered and it was here that our outdoor kitchen was located. We'd have to carry the propane by hand, but still this was a huge luxury for us. I was willing to do any carrying necessary to have it, and I quickly became an expert at the technicalities involved. We did not have indoor plumbing, but we did have a proper outhouse and an additional shed to put our extra clothing and other items. Our home itself was small and did not have any built-in storage space. Nevertheless, this was definitely a step up, and I was thrilled.

One day as we were making our way down the hill towards our new home, Daren happened to notice one tree moving just beside our house. He silenced my chattering and put his arm in front of me to bring me to a halt. Just then a bear stepped right out in front of us not more than ten yards away. For a moment, we were all shocked at seeing each other. It didn't really occur to me to be scared; the bear looked so natural being there. Then Daren told me to back up slowly and then run. He followed. The bear did not. He was probably as shocked as we were.

Later, when we returned clanging all manner of kitchen utensils, we realized that the outdoor kitchen would have to become an indoor one. Though there was no food outside, the smell of dishwater had attracted the bear. We closed in the side-deck and extended it, making a full little house with a living room, small kitchen area and wood stove surrounded with lots of windows and sliding glass doors to the outside world.

Daren and I discovered a small spring close to our house. We did not have the water tested, but it tasted fine, so we began to use it for our watering needs. Water still had to be hauled to the upper property where the garden was located, but this at least made our work here a little easier.

For summers, Daren set up a little place for us to bathe, directing the spring into a tub, which we could get into. He took old stumps of logs and placed flowers and greenery on them, a bit of soap, some shampoo. The first time we got in there it was a shock! The water was freezing cold, likely coming from the snow capped mountains just above us. But we so enjoyed our pool. No one could see us and we could frolic outside without concern for our modesty. Only scantily dressed, we'd make our meals on the deck and enjoy the summer weather. Spring and summer were the easiest times on the land. We did not have to protect ourselves from the cold. It was the winter that was the hardest.

The winters were cold, often dropping to 35 below zero. We would have to keep waking up to feed the fire that kept us warm. We only had a limited amount of propane and often had to choose between cooking our food and heating our room. No matter how cold it was we had to keep the window near the refrigerator open. It is not safe to keep a propane fridge in the house because of the risk of carbon monoxide poisoning.

One year, we didn't have wood cut before the first snow and ended up with damp wood, which is very difficult to light, and even harder with fingers nearly frozen from cold. Another year, I had the wood cut to the wrong size and it didn't fit in the stove.

Sometimes it would be so cold we'd go to sleep with long underwear, pants, several socks, sweatshirt, hat, gloves and a winter coat. I have never experienced such cold before or since in my entire life. It was too cold to go to the bathroom outside at night, so Daren rigged up a 5-gallon bucket with a toilet seat on top in another room. One of us would empty it in the morning.

We carried in everything we needed from the top of the hill. Everything from groceries to propane tanks came down that hill. My brother gave us an alternator that could be hooked up to a car battery to give us some power. At night my big treat was to watch an episode or two of "Friends" on DVD with a little RV DVD player we had purchased. We never had enough power to watch an entire movie, and there were many movies we never saw the end of. I enjoyed having a little bit of power at night to play some music, have enough light to read by or watch a little something. But that meant that one of us had to carry that car battery up and down the hill to charge it.

As critters figured out we were living in their area, they began to find their way into the house. Virtually all the socks, shirts, and underwear stored in our dressers were filled with holes the mice made at night. But unlike my early days, I didn't crumble. I could take these things more in stride, though being cold at night was the hardest.

Through the seasons, I would routinely go to my "office" to continue building our small business. I enjoyed myself there and felt I was creating something reflective of us and of what I thought we wanted to do in the world.

As people heard Daren was teaching again, the invitations began to pour in. Thinking this was a good thing, I encouraged him to take the work. We could use the income to pay off our debts and continue to live. What I did not recognize was that this was not what Daren wanted. He had gone to the land for a reason. He didn't have much work for a reason. It was not something he wanted at this point in his life. He wanted time for self-reflection–time to work the land, to read, to study, to be with his son and granddaughter. He took the work for me, but he was unhappy doing it. For me, the times away teaching were the happiest memories I had. They were the times I most enjoyed and treasured. I had no idea he was not enjoying it, and was in fact doing it to please me.

Daren's true dream for us was that I would embrace a life centered around the land. He hoped I would make our new place a home for us; I would devote my time and attention here, cooking, gardening, and attending to the house and chores, while he did the same. As it became increasingly clear I was moving out into the world with my own teaching and our business, he became more distant. Eventually, his disappointment surfaced. Though part of me knew this was the issue, I didn't want to know.

I was finding my place in the world, a place where I felt empowered and able to contribute in a significant way. The thought of being on the land did not inspire me at all. Perhaps this was due to the fact that we were in different stages of our lives. Daren had already made his mark in the world. He had done it and knew what it was all about. I had not. I felt the world was still waiting for me.

This is a question many women face. Do we give up our life's purpose for the love of a relationship? Or do we make our self-expression in the world a priority and allow everything to flow from there? And if we do the latter, will we lose the love we so desperately want? Even if our life's purpose is to raise children and be a good mother, this can be an issue. Do we put our priority on motherhood or on being a good wife and lover? As any mother knows, the two will not always coincide and can be a source of conflict.

THE TABLES ARE TURNED

Those questions were no different for me. In my previous relationship, Steve could not be what I wanted. *Now, I could not be what Daren wanted.* In a different arena to be sure, but the general theme was there. The tables were turned and it felt bad to be the one who could not measure up to my partner's wants and needs without compromising my own. The way I had created my life was the only way I knew to make an almost untenable lifestyle work for me. To give it up felt akin to willfully wounding myself.

From Daren's perspective, it probably seemed I had broken our agreement. I had said I loved him and wanted to be with him. When I started to have my own life, to teach and travel, I no longer fit his picture of an ideal mate. Perhaps he took that to mean I didn't love him. When I began to try to better manage our finances, our daily logistics, or participate in common decisions, I was seen as stripping his masculinity. The more I came into my own, the more I was perceived as unloving.

I wanted Daren to see I still loved him even though I wasn't exactly the person he'd hoped for. I contributed to our relationship in a different way than he had hoped, but I did contribute. I earned money so we could live on the land, helping his dream happen. But in his human disappointment, Daren saw his dream fading before his eyes, and likely me as the culprit.

So, I tried to become what Daren wanted. I tried to fit myself into the picture he'd created of his perfect partner because I wanted his love. I willed myself to stay home and focus on the household. I did my best to do it all the "right" way–the way someone excited to take care of a home would have done it. I tried to pretend this was all I wanted, to disappear into a simple life in the wilderness. But the real me kept popping out. I'd come up with great ideas to grow our business, think of people I could call and worry about details not covered. So after I'd done all my chores at home, I'd try to get to the office and do all my work there as well. As a result, Daren and I had less time to spend together, which drove us apart even more.

CHAPTER TWENTY-TWO

I N THE MIDST of our unfolding life, it never occurred to me the dynamics we were playing out were not only personal, but universal. Entrenched in the minutiae of my every-day life, I had little or no ability to access a more objective perspective. I did not see how my own internal energetic tendencies were manifesting through the relationship. Had I been able to create more internal balance, I might have experienced less push/pull between Daren and me.

In order to understand our basic patterns, we need to first understand how two basic polar energies manifest within us, and how internal tendencies towards imbalance often echo through any relationship we are in.

EXTERNAL DYNAMICS AND INTERNAL IMBALANCES

Polarity is at the core of all creation. Chinese call it *yin* and *yang*. In psychology, *anima* and *animus*. In yoga, *shakti* and *shiva* or *ida* and *pingala*. From one comes two, and from two multitudes of forms. Everything that exists in form, from the subtlest to the grossest, exists in polarity. Electrical and magnetic energies manifest through positive and negative currents. Biological systems, like our heart and lungs, manifest through balance of expansion and contraction.

In the same way, psychological energies manifest through willful, assertive attitudes and more surrendered, receptive ways of being. Yin is the inclusive, yielding or surrendered force. It is often associated with the feminine principle. Yang, associated with the masculine principle, is a contracted, aggressive, structured and willful force. Though we have a biological gender, these same two elemental forces exist within each one of us. When we learn to create an ideal internal balance between these polar forces, we set the stage for these two forces to merge together, creating internal wholeness—oneness.

Though we don't always recognize it, these polar forces are complementary. The opposing muscle actions of contraction and release *both* contribute to one unified action called movement. Inhalation and exhalation, though seemingly at odds, both contribute to the unified function called breathing. In the same way, the polar forces within each of us are meant to be complementary. They both contribute to one central function which is self-actualization; becoming a whole, healthy person expressing their full potential in the world.

Hatha yoga centers on creating this inner experience of balance. Once we create that experience within us, we bring wholeness to all the experiences of our lives. In fact, the root word "Ha" of "hatha" actually means sun. The root word "tha" of "hatha" means moon. Yoga means union. Hatha yoga is about bringing together and balancing our masculine (sun) and feminine (moon) energies in such a way that they lead back to an experience of our own wholeness.

Many spiritual traditions work with energies in various ways to create optimal internal balance of yin and yang or "ha" and "tha" as a gateway to realizing oneness.

ELEMENTAL POLARITY IN A RELATIONSHIP

In the quest for internal yin-yang balance and ultimate wholeness, we can learn a lot about our inner energetic landscape by looking at the way we relate to others. We might often notice, for example, that we tend to gravitate towards qualities or aspects in another rather than developing them in ourselves. This initial attraction may be a reflection of our own inner urge to seek balance. The more that balance has not been found internally, the more we will tend, albeit unconsciously, to seek it externally. Conversely, the more internally balanced we are, the less our attractions will be driven by filling what is unfinished or undeveloped within us.

That is not to say that we cannot have complementary balance in a relationship. But if we are *depending* on the other to fulfill an undeveloped part of us, we may inadvertently cut off

our own development and eventually resent the balancing qualities the other is trying to bring us. Those very same qualities,
at some point down the line, may become a source of conflict
and irritation where they were once a source of attraction. We
begin to see their qualities as an attempt to change who we are
or make us wrong, when in fact they are simply mirroring the
aspects of ourselves we may not have developed.

GAINING INSIGHT INTO OUR ELEMENTAL ENERGIES

We both have feminine (yin) and masculine (yang) energies operating within us at different times and in different situations. But
overall, we may notice a subtle reliance on one type of energy
or way of being over another. In order to better understand our
predominating elemental strategy, we'll take each of these energies to their extremes. Of course each one has positive, useful
qualities as well. Yin energy is soft, receptive, giving, and yielding. It has a nurturing and accepting quality to it. But in excess,
that giving can become over-giving. Yang energy is directed,
willful and goal-oriented. But in excess can become constricted,
demanding and controlling.

Excess yin and yang employ a different strategy for achiev-
ing the same goal. A goal that we can call union, wholeness or
love. This strategy is one that manifests in the way we interact
with others, but is rooted in our own internal energetic strengths
and weaknesses.

EXCESS YIN ENERGY

Excess yin energy seeks union or wholeness through merging—
through becoming what the other wants. They seek love through
submerging the self. Not only through receptivity, but often
through a complete loss of self.

In the movie "Coming to America" with Eddie Murphy,
Eddie's character is contemplating an arranged marriage to
a beautiful woman. Upon first meeting her he asks her what
her interests are and she replies, "Whatever you like." He asks
her what she wants to do in life and she replies, "Whatever you

want." Finally he asks her to bark like a dog and cluck like a chicken while hopping on one foot in a circle—and she does!

While I'm not suggesting we would go that far, an excess yin personality does try to be whatever the other wants. When asked their opinion or to make a decision, they will try to figure out what the other person really wants and give that answer. Or they will simply say something like, "I don't know, what do you want?"

The excess yin is seeking love through approval and doing the right things in other people's eyes. They are about service, but getting validation through that service. "If I give myself to you completely, if I do everything for you, then you'll love me and I'll experience wholeness." Therefore their partner's needs, children's needs, family's needs, society's needs—everyone else's needs but their own will tend to take precedence.

Because they are driven by getting love through being of service to others, they have a very hard time saying no, or rocking the boat in any way. Even when they know something is clearly not right, they will hesitate to say it outright. They might hint or suggest, but will rarely take clear and direct opposition to anything that is being said or done—even if it would be to their benefit. Instead of saying, "Hey, you're going the wrong way." They might say something like, "Are you sure we're going the right way?"

The excess yin has difficulty setting limits. So in order to save themselves from a complete inner collapse, they will often become passive-aggressive. Passive-aggressive behavior is a "no" that has not been given the room to speak. But actions speak louder than words; and while words overtly say "yes," actions will covertly say "no."

An excess yin would rather hurt themselves than create confrontation or conflict because conflict is seen as a threat to love. They will either not speak their real feelings or will soften what they say so much they do not find self-expression through their words. What they are really trying to say is hidden under layers, which require much deciphering and interpretation.

Unexpressed feelings will tend to "leak" out in little digs, cold silences, bouts of withdrawal and self-pity. People who step into the presence of an excess yin who is upset, can't miss the message being sent. Something is wrong. The other will often have to guess what it is and try to figure it out. If they ask the excess yin what is wrong, they will often get, "Nothing is wrong!" and a bright, fake smile. This leaves the people around them feeling like detectives trying to decipher what they've done or not done to incur this very uncomfortable "cold shoulder." Because the excess yin cannot clearly state their preferences, they end up trying to communicate their needs through guilt. They are the originators of the "guilt trip."

In short, an excess yin will tend to suppress what they need, not speak up, and then when they don't get what they really wanted (because they didn't speak up), they feel bad about it. They feel forgotten and unloved. It becomes a self-perpetuating cycle. When emotions finally become so strong they cannot be held back, they often overpower reason and logic, creating the appearance of being overly emotional or dramatic.

An excess yin is about love and service–but with expectation. It all sounds and looks really good. But he or she does not give just to give. There are conditions and expectations of return attached. "If I behave this way, you are supposed to do this or that." The expectation of return might be approval, recognition or attention. It is an exchange model. It is an underground form of control. But it is a method of controlling and securing love nonetheless.

EXCESS YANG ENERGY

On the other hand, an excess yang's strategy to create oneness is through authority. The overt use of control, structure and hierarchy. Think of a troop commander. In the act of one person leading and the others following, a common direction is created–union.

The problem with this model in a relationship is that it can run counter to the principle of equal expression. In order for this to work, the leader needs to have the follower follow their rules. "I tell you what to do and you do it." When the other says, "Can't we talk about it or both be involved in the decision-making?" the excess yang will often see the other as a problem or a troublemaker because they are not following along with the plan. "You are deliberately working against my efforts to create union." If the other were to follow the plan, there would be no dis-harmony, there would simply be a common movement towards a desired goal and outcome.

Any questioning, suggestions or input are taken as a loss of confidence in the yang's ability to lead. From a yang person's point of view, "The plan is you follow my plan and then we'll become one." In this model for union, somebody will often lose their voice in the relationship because an excess yang will tend to make unilateral decisions without including the other. From their point of view this is what they are supposed to do. "I'm supposed to make decisions and you're supposed to follow along and help me. I have a perfect right."

A yang will often tell others how to do it better and often needs to have the last word on everything—even if they have to contradict what they said just moments before. They will say things like, "That's not how you do it. What are you doing it like that for? Do it like this." No matter how well the other might do something, they always manage to find something wrong.

In contrast, an excess yin will praise even when it is unwarranted. They might think of telling the other how to do it better, might even hint at it, but will not come right out and say it. Or they might let the other one mess it up first and then make a suggestion. But even then it might come out as, "Maybe you want to think about...."

When their opinions or methods are questioned, an excess yang often takes a more aggressive attitude that might look like, "What would you know? This is how I/we do it. If you don't like it, leave." My way or the highway.

On the other hand, when an excess yin's methods or opinions are questioned, they will tend to crumble, back off and question themselves. "Maybe you are right, maybe I'm not doing it right. Maybe I don't know what I'm talking about." Or, even if they disagree, they will keep the peace by suppressing their own voice.

Yang is more logic and reason based, while the yin is more feeling based. A yin's priority is to make sure everyone feels good. That is what gives them value. A yang's priority is to make sure outcomes are attained through directed attention, focus and discipline. They get value from performance and outcome. "I did well. I produced well. I created good results." That is desirable, but ideally includes the means as well as the end.

In communication a yin will talk about feelings. A yang wants to know the bottom line, "Get to the point. What do you want? What's your problem?"

Yang is very good at caring for themselves. They will attend to themselves and if they have something left over, they will care for the other. They will do things when it is convenient for them, when they "feel like it" and can get to it. Yin is all about the other person, "As long as the people around me are happy, I am happy." This person will tend to burn out in their concern for others and then resent it.

The yang has something very valuable to contribute to the excess yin who tends to give up all personal need and self-care for others. Likewise, the yin can contribute unselfishness to the yang who can appear not to think about others in the process of caring for themselves.

Excess yang can move from protective towards controlling. The protective instinct feels good, but can often come with an underlying attitude that, "You are not competent enough to take care of yourself." The other needs caring for and watching over because they cannot be trusted to take care of themselves, "I know what you need. I know you better than you know yourself."

IT'S NOT ABOUT GENDER

While it is easy to think that we are describing men and women, these are actually qualities both of us have whether we realize it or not. For example, as women we have many "rules" and "structures" within which our partner is supposed to behave. We have strong ideas about how things "should" be done around the house, with our children, our families and more.

We may take on a more yang position covertly through treating the other like a child—in a condescending fashion—as if they cannot be left to manage things on their own without our help. We might say things like, "Someone has to be responsible." Or "Someone has to be the grown-up." But what we don't recognize is that we are in part contributing to the dynamic through the role we are playing. By holding one pole strongly we encourage the other to settle into the opposite.

Sometimes men take on certain yin energies. They may not be emotional, but they may shy away from making decisions or be more passive in certain arenas. They may abdicate much of their power and instead look to their partner to set the direction and tone of the relationship. Yet at the same time they may manifest passive aggressive behaviors in an attempt to find their own internal balance—which they cannot seem to find any other way. That would be an example of yin energy manifesting itself.

These patterns do not just play themselves out in love relationships. We can see them in parent and child, boss and employee, and even in organizations. A more yin organization is a horizontal organization in which everyone is included in the decision making process. A more yang organization is the more traditional vertical style in which decisions are made at the top and underlings are expected to follow. Neither one is a perfect model. For a while the trend was to move towards a more horizontal, inclusive model (yin) until it became apparent that inclusiveness and information gathering still had to be balanced with final decision-making and visionary direction (yang) in order to keep organizations productive.

FROM OPPOSITION TO BALANCE TO WHOLENESS

Whether in an organization or personal relationship, the opposite pole often appears as an obstruction. We may feel we cannot be who we are. Or it may appear that the other person is working against the togetherness we are trying to create through our elemental strategy. The authoritative yang may appear as an aggressive and unwanted contrast to the yin's style of creating wholeness through inclusiveness and receptivity. The yin's feeling-based style may be irritating to the yang, who wants to garner value by getting things done. That's often how conflict shows up in relationship. We dismiss the other's elemental energy and with it, we dismiss the key they offer to our own integration and wholeness.

While these two energies are seemingly at odds with each other, we can begin to see how both poles could work together to create a more unified, self-actualized person—which would then contribute to a more unified and less-polarized relationship. For example, making choices solely for our own benefit (yang) is only one half of the picture. Only doing what works for the other (yin) compromises personal energy and boundaries. But a combination of the two in harmony moves us towards being a healthy, whole person in our own right. We can see how this would automatically contribute to a more harmonious relationship.

Each pole has its strengths and weaknesses. But its weaknesses can be solved by integrating elements from the opposite pole. If we could recognize in what areas we are excessively yin or yang and balance out by moving towards the center and incorporating elements (not the extremes) of the opposite pole, we can find inner wholeness. A whole person is able to let go of boundaries in service to the other, but also able to set them when necessary. They are able to ask and listen, but also to tell and direct. They can take a more passive, receptive role, but can also be assertive and action-oriented. They can value others' feelings but also perform and create desired outcomes. They are at times dependent, but also able to be independent.

This is the place where opposites no longer struggle with each other, just as the dark of night does not struggle with the light of day. Each is allowed its place through the allowance of its complementary opposite. Here oneness can be perceived beyond what at first seems to be conflict and separation. This is where yin and yang are no longer seen as two halves, but as two elemental energies that serve one function–wholeness. Just as breath in and breath out both serve one function–life.

In psychology or yoga circles it is often said we need to be whole before we can be fully in a relationship with another. To me, this is one map that can help us do this. And it is pretty simple to remember. Whatever it is we always do to excess, we need to begin to bring in just a little of the opposite. Not so much that we swing to the other side, but just enough that we begin to move towards the center point between the internal poles of male and female energies.

Now it must be said, not all relationships manifest both poles. Sometimes couples, siblings, parents and children or bosses and employees will find wholeness through sameness. Homogeneousness. Then, we might see that *both* people are excessive yin or yang. This, of course, is not in balance either. In that case, both parties need to balance by integrating the opposite elemental energy within themselves.

Sometimes, though it appears that both people involved are homogeneous, one may actually be a yin in yang disguise. Looking for unity and sameness, one will take on the qualities of the other in order to create the sense of unity, merging and acceptance they are seeking. Children may spout the same thoughts and opinions as their parents and may even mimic their behavior. One partner will often do the same for the other; hence the sometimes shocking changes in dress, attitudes, interests and behaviors of people we know when they fall in love.

ENERGY SEEKS BALANCE

The nature of energy is to seek balance, homeostasis. What we often don't realize is when we bring an excess yin pattern to a relationship, we are actually creating the environment where the other person is likely to be more yang to instinctively balance us out.

Let's imagine we are standing face to face with a partner about two feet away from us. If our partner were to move towards us quickly and unexpectedly, what would we instinctively do? Most of us would have the impulse to move backwards—right? I suggest this impulse to move backwards is an instinctive, intuitive balancing process we don't even think about. If someone moves aggressively into our space, we tend to balance by pulling back a little. Or, if we tend to hold back, the other will tend to move into our space. I suggest this doesn't just happen at the level of the body, it also happens energetically in a relationship. Of course this is not always true, especially when two dominant energies meet each other. But it is often the case.

What does this mean for us? It means that if we are excessively yang and push past the center point into the other person's space, they will tend to take a more yin stance to balance out the whole picture. If we are excessively yin and tend to retreat far back, the yang will naturally tend to move into the vacant space we have left to fill it. All in an intuitive search for balance. We sometimes see this effect in parent child relationships as well. In order to establish some kind of balance, children may polarize to the other side in a way that looks like it is against us. This could simply be the outcome of an intuitive attempt to bring energetic equilibrium to the relationship. While many parents will view this as a behavior problem, it may be that the more we come to center, the more children will tend to do the same.

If our polar stance influences how the other person shows up in a relationship, this also means that as we change our standpoint in the relationship we can often effect a change in the other person as well (though we don't want to depend on it).

The less of a polar extreme we take, the less the other will take as well. And if we were to be completely centered and balanced in ourselves because our inner energies were neither driving us forward or holding us back, we would be creating an optimum environment for the relationship to be balanced as well. No guarantees, but the best possible situation where push and pull would be least likely to occur. Because we'd be standing in ourselves, the other would not need to push into our space or pull back. They would be in the best possible position to access their own inner balance as well.

This kind of re-adjustment in a relationship takes time. When we suddenly shift our way of being, it temporarily throws off the balance of the relationship. The other person can be taken aback and react to the sudden change. That is why a slow, steady movement towards a more centered way of being can often be the better strategy to avoid alienating the other person or leaving them lost, insecure or even angry and betrayed. I liken this to a shared balance pose in gymnastics. If one of the pair makes a sudden unexpected movement, both parties will be thrown off balance. But if one slowly and deliberately moves in a certain direction and allows the other time to adjust from moment to moment along the way, balance can be maintained while the "shape" of the relationship changes. This includes working at the other person's edge so that they are aware that changes are happening, but the changes are not so intense or threatening as to bring up their guard.

WHAT MIGHT UNION IN A RELATIONSHIP LOOK LIKE?

What does it feel like when we are balanced in ourselves and therefore in the relationship? Union in a relationship feels effortless. There is no struggle. The creative tension between the two poles is what holds the relationship together, as opposed to our individual will or struggle.

To understand this more fully, let's imagine that this time we are facing a partner and, clasped wrist to wrist, we are leaning away from each other. Once the balance is found through the dynamic tension between each pole, there is sense of ease— a sweet spot. Can we sense that at this balance point between the two, there is no longer an experience of "two-ness"? Even though two poles make up the unity, what is felt no longer feels like two things, but as one thing called balance. It is a place where no struggle or effort is necessary. It naturally arises out of the perfect interplay of yin and yang.

As long as the two are in conflict, we can never create true union. The poles are not working together for a common unity of balance. Rather, each is in conflict with the other for control and power. Conflict induces struggle. Now, both parties have to work hard to create balance. This is one reason a relationship starts to feel difficult and challenging.

This is what was happening with Daren and me. Rather than viewing the other's needs as one aspect of a whole picture, we began to see the one holding the opposite point of view as the problem. We were so busy struggling for the power to have our needs met, we lost our natural union and balance. Natural polarity turning against itself was the true problem. When two hands of one body fight with each another, the body loses no matter who wins. In the same way, the body of our relationship was losing because the two parts that made it up were in conflict. No matter who "won," the relationship would lose. The balance and harmony would be lost. Only in changing our perspective and seeing each other as a natural part of the equation would we be able to re-establish balance. We needed to move from "conflict" back to "complementary."

CHAPTER TWENTY-THREE

IN MY RELATIONSHIP with Daren, I saw myself as the nice, sweet, kind, giving person who had done what she was supposed to do; give herself fully without any thought of personal needs. I thought by giving more and more and more (excess yin) I was helping create union. "I'm giving. I'm surrendering. I'm letting go," I told myself. That is spiritual. That is what I'm *supposed* to do. I thought of Daren as the "bad" one who had primarily been concerned with his own wants and needs and who had not included me in any decision-making processes. I was wrong.

It wasn't that I was seeking union and he wasn't. We were *both* seeking union, but in *different ways*. As an excess yin, I was seeking union through acceptance and approval. I got this through service to others and suppressing my own desires and needs. Daren was seeking union by setting the direction and wanting to create union through my following him. We were both trying to do the same thing, but each of us, based on our conditioning, and the way it affected our inner energies, had differing strategies to accomplish this.

Each of us, being individually out of balance, was seeking union, but only through our own pole; him through a yang strategy, me through a yin. When I eventually recognized this, it gave me compassion and understanding that Daren truly wanted to create union, he just had a strategy that was completely different from mine. He genuinely believed he was doing the best for us by taking the lead, just as I truly believed I was contributing to unity by giving up my own voice. That did not detract from the fact that he was a kind, loving, wonderful man.

Neither of us was able to recognize that we *both* needed to be comfortable with our inner yin and yang and able to flow back and forth between both roles in the relationship at different times and under different circumstances. But neither of us could see it. We were too busy grappling with the conflict our relationship was creating to see that the tension was in fact an opportunity to wake up.

IN THE NAME OF UNION WE UNWITTINGLY PREVENT IT

Something that most of us never realize is that by giving too much in the name of union, we can actually *prevent* it. The first time I recognized this was groundbreaking for me. My attitude in a relationship and in fact in my whole life had been, "I'll do whatever you want. Be whatever you want. I will give myself to this relationship totally and the more I can sublimate my own needs to the needs of the relationship, the more likely I will be to make it work."

Let's imagine we are facing a partner as before, but this time our palms are pressed against the other's palms and both sets of arms are stretched overhead, creating a teepee shape. Imagine both partners are leaning against one another in balance.

Now, let us say we are excess yin in the relationship, and the centerpoint is the midline between both partners. As an excess feminine energy, we would metaphorically give ourselves up so completely that we would be caving our body weight into the center and maybe even beyond as we give up our personal will and power to the other. We are being what the other wants, giving up our voice, our wants and our needs. But that also means we are effectively no longer holding ourselves up. That means all the extra weight now falls upon our partner. To them, we might suddenly feel like "dead weight" when just moments ago, the effort to remain in balance was much easier.

Assuming energy wants to seek balance, can we see how the other person almost has *no choice* but to push back to maintain balance? And can we see how that would appear to the yin person as their partner being overly yang? Without recognizing our part in the scenario, we could say they are the problem, but actually, we could be the one creating the scenario by excessively leaning in, giving them few other options besides to push back.

This is what I did with Daren. I was so convinced he had been the problem, when I, through my own patterns of excess yin had been a significant cause of the pattern we created. This was a huge eye-opener for me.

Now notice how it might feel for the excess yin who is leaning into the center. As he or she begins to lean inward in an abdication of self, they find themselves in an increasingly precarious, ungrounded, and unsafe position. The more they lean inward, the more they lose control. With it comes a progressive downward spiraling loss of self that seems to gain more and more momentum. I experienced this as well. It can be terrifying to find oneself in this kind of an emotional freefall.

What Daren and I experienced is fairly typical of many relationships. But the same dynamic in its extreme form can lead to abusive relationships. As I've said before, abusive relationships are not a safe place to practice or learn. The best thing we can do in this kind of a situation is employ the yang energy of getting out.

YANG DYNAMICS IN RELATIONSHIP

What about the excess yang? How does that work? This can best be understood by imagining both partners leaning *away* from one another in balance, clasping wrist to wrist at shoulder height.

The yang energy will try to pull the other towards them as they attempt to get the other person to move with them in their chosen direction. As the yang pulls what might the partner being pulled instinctively do to maintain balance or to keep some semblance of who they are? Resist? Try to lean back away from their partner? Can we see how that induces conflict and struggle in the relationship as one tries to pull and other tries to balance things out with resistance? Now the one resisting looks like the "bad" person; the one who doesn't want to go along. But they are not bad, they are simply trying to correct an imbalance in the relationship.

Another common shape that happens in this dynamic is that a yin, in an attempt to hold ground against the yang's pulling, jackknifes. The upper body goes with the yang, but the buttocks and legs hold back to provide counterforce. Let's describe the body shape this way and see what insight we gain: On the surface, the yin appears to be following along and allowing themselves to be pulled, evidenced by their arms and torso moving forward. But underneath, the yin is not following along. Their hips are pulling back and their legs are trying to hold ground.

What are we describing? A passive-aggressive stance. Up top (on the surface) the yin is going along but that appearance is suppressing what is really going on underneath, which is resistance. The yin *appears* to be submitting, but in order for them to keep any sense of self, they *have* to hold back. That doesn't make the yin a bad person, they are not weak or manipulative for being passive aggressive. This may simply seem like the only way the yin can create any sort of balance for themselves and for the relationship in the face of excess yang.

Another common theme when the yang pulls yin in a certain direction is that yin is pulled off balance and is now dependent on yang to establish balance for them. This can manifest as dependency or neediness. Now that the yin is off balance, whether through their own doing or their partner's, they need to somehow find a sense of self. They will often try to find it in the other, since that seems to be the only source of stability available.

The dynamics we're seeing are not a result of ourselves or our partner being good or bad, but simply a reflection of our own internal dynamics being reflected in an external relationship. The external can literally be a visual representation of how yin and yang energies are operating inside of us.

Yin/Yang Dynamics with Daren

Before I ever met Daren, my primary elemental energy was excess yin. From a young age I learned to do and be whatever the other wanted (at least on the surface of things). That is not to say that I was a yin all the time and under all circumstances. Actually, when it came to work and finances, even life structure, I would say I was more yang. I expected basic life needs and responsibilities should be attended to in a certain way. I had ambition and goals I wanted to achieve.

But living on the land was an extreme yin experience. My need to achieve goals and have a solid and dependable life structure could scarcely be attained given the reality of living on the land. It seemed to me nothing could be counted on. There was no stability or foundation. There was no plan that could be relied on. We couldn't plan to get to town at a certain time or guarantee that we'd even be able to pay our bills. Nothing was certain. The more yin my external life became, the more yang I became to try to balance it out. I tried to become more organized, more together, make more money, and direct Daren and the kids to be more "responsible" in my eyes; moving towards a more stable life through goals I had set for us.

But, from my perspective, the more yang I became, the more yin Daren got. The more I tried to get him to save money, the more he seemed to spend it. The more I tried to build our business, the more he appeared to resist my efforts. If we were to use this model, it was not that he was working against me, he was simply playing the opposite end to my pole.

My extreme tightness, something I had never before experienced in myself, shocked me. "How can I be so inflexible?" I thought. I always was the sweet-natured person who would go along with pretty much anything. I thought I was finding out that underneath all that I was just a nasty person and had never realized it. It wasn't until later that I realized the extreme yin environment of no limits, no boundaries, no plan, no organization caused me to try to balance things out by becoming more yang. Because the environment was *extreme* yin, I became an *extreme* yang.

During this time, demand for me to teach on my own was growing. Using the argument that we needed the money, I accepted the offers. Seeing this as the "responsible" thing to do–and also out of taking care of myself (more yang qualities), I accepted. Daren said nothing. He simply withdrew more and more into his own world (yin).

While on the road, I discovered that this new excess yang part of me also contained a positive side. When tempered, it contained a strong and self-assured part of me that had been forged not only from teaching, but from the hardship I had faced on the land.

At times I would express this new part of myself in the relationship. When skillfully done, usually when I had just returned home and was resting in a more centered place between yin and yang, it worked. We got along well. I wasn't afraid of Daren's disapproval and could lightly own my own needs while caring for him. The key was "lightly." I wasn't trying to convince him of my point of view or trying to get his approval. What I wanted or needed was simply stated as a neutral fact, a given, to be factored in with all the other details we needed to manage. But as soon as I started to look to him to sanction my needs, or get him to be a certain way from a "pushy" point of view, the balance was thrown off and that sweet spot of balanced union was lost.

Even though I was moving towards extreme yang in terms of organizing our lives and trying, without success, to create some structure out of the untamed lifestyle of the land, I still had excess yin tendencies on the personal level. I could see that my yang attempts to lead us to a grounded lifestyle were creating resistance and passive aggressive behavior on the other side.

Recognizing my new strategy was actually alienating my partner, I went back to my old strategy– being an excess yin. I would give up my own wants and needs and do what the other wanted. Then I would be able to secure the love I wanted and things would be okay. The yang tendencies were still there, but I suppressed them. Instead of moving to the center, where I might have continued to organize, but from a more inclusive and relaxed stance (incorporating the best of yin and yang), I did my best to push down any of my personal will. I made myself go underground, as yins do, in order to keep the peace—so my partner would be happy. He could once again take the yang stance in the relationship—*his* most comfortable mode of being.

As I did this I began to spiral downwards. An excess Yin, completely leaning on her partner, loses her sense of self. She has none of her own footing and can quickly sink downward into dark despair, having given up her will to the other.

I became one person when I was teaching, and another at home. There I kept myself as small and insignificant as I possibly could. I didn't want to rock the boat. I pretended to enjoy all the things Daren wanted and put my real self away. I suppressed any differing opinions or feelings about anything we were doing. I told myself to keep my mouth shut, even if I disagreed with a decision. It was better to be quiet than risk displeasure.

I hid my successes. I hid my true thoughts and feelings. I became a shell of who I once was, going through the motions as the picture perfect partner, but my spirit was dying. Daren did not break me. I don't believe anyone can unless we give them permission to do so. I broke myself in order to be lovable to him.

CHAPTER TWENTY-FOUR

ROUND THIS TIME I noticed a recurring pain in my low back. No matter what I did, it didn't go away. I went to the chiropractor and it helped for a time, but over the next year the pain became steadily worse. Still, I forced myself to do my chores, trying to subjugate my body to my will, just as I was forcing in so many other ways. By this time, Daren and I were spending less and less time together, and when we did, we hardly spoke. There was a sea of disappointment and unspoken resentment between us that could not be breached.

Just as I had built resentment for Steve not being who I wanted, Daren was beginning to resent me for not being the partner he thought he was getting. In the mornings, Daren awoke early and left me in the house on my own. Though I was going through all the right motions, he knew my heart was not in it. My body language and energy said it all. I did what he wanted on the surface, but underneath my resistance and resentment was palpable. Neither of us was happy, and neither of us would win in this scenario. My unexpressed thoughts and feelings could only find balance in the form of a yin's passive resistance, and I'm sure that was not nice to be around.

Considering my back just a nuisance, I continued with chores. Sometimes the pain was so bad I'd have to take a rest and lie on my back every five minutes or so. But it wasn't just the pain in my body that was growing. It was a deep pain in my soul. I was now estranged from the one person I was here for. And not only that, I had given myself up for his love and now could not find *me*. My body was present, but I had gone far away. I had gone so far away from myself, even I didn't know who I was. I had lost any sense of my center and could not find it.

When we hide parts of ourselves, the danger is that, when sought, they are not so easily found. I began to fall into a deep depression. I felt alone and isolated with no one to turn to for solace. I remember sobbing alone in the cabin, crying out to God for help. I felt lost, alone. This is an excerpt from my journal:

I feel so sad. I'm crying. How did I end up here so alone, no one to talk to? No one to be my friend. I need help. Please God, help me. I have no place to turn. Nowhere to go. No way out. How did I get here? How have I come so far down? I don't know. And I can't see how I will ever get out. How I'll ever be the happy, sweet, joyous person I once was. All I can see is pain, unending pain. I feel like a drowning island slowly going under. Trying to keep on a good face while I slowly die. Is this growing up? Maybe I just have to learn to live with the reality of what is without wishing myself dead. I can't help it. When I see an eternity of this life laid out before me, I just want to give up. I'm losing my will to live. I'm losing my belief that I will ever find happiness. I see a life before me, isolated and alone. And if I can't take it now, how will I live through the rest of my lifetime? What an irony to think oneself in a relationship and yet feel more alone than I ever have.

Though I don't believe I would have done it, I thought about taking my own life. I felt I did not have any options. I could not leave Daren. I had already left one long-term relationship and I didn't want to see myself as a failure. But the truth was I was miserable staying. Not only did I feel unable to fully and openly pursue my life's purpose, I had completely compromised myself in the name of love. I truly didn't belong here and I knew it–I just wasn't willing to admit it out loud. Yes, we'd created a more livable life. I had learned to make the best of it, and in a certain sense, had even mastered it. But it wasn't me. It never would be. It was simply something I had managed to tolerate with greater skill.

The nature here was breathtaking. I had experienced so many magical moments in our cabin together. The picture of our little house filled with candlelight underneath an explosion of stars, the sound of water rushing by as we lay in bed, memories of us laughing, cooking, even dancing by the side of the road as we waited, sometimes for hours, for a car to come by.

But still, they could not outweigh a truth. I was reluctant to admit it, even to myself, because if I did it would mean I had again failed. It would mean the destiny, the storybook tale of Daren and me that I had put so much faith in, was a farce. It was just something I had made up. And all the time and energy I had invested in it would have been pointless. This I simply could not face. If I stayed, I would be unhappy. If I left, I'd have to admit everything that had come before was not real. I felt there was no way out.

THE PENDULUM SWINGS

I came into the relationship as an excess yin. From what I gathered, Daren believed he should be a yang in relationship, so I fit the mold perfectly. Then the life on the land pushed me the opposite way and I had a glimpse into another side of me—but the extreme side. This pushed Daren to the yin side. Finally, I tried to alleviate the situation by going back to who I had been—a nice little yin girl. And I use the word "girl" deliberately.

But it was just a cover up for a change already happening inside me. The yang part of me would no longer be denied. She wanted input. She wanted a say. She wanted to be included. She wasn't happy just to follow along anymore. The more it was suppressed, the stronger it showed up as resistance to Daren's yang style.

From this point of view, we each appeared to the other as the cause of our problems and our conflict. If we had only been the "same," I thought, it might have been easier. This is probably why many couples become homogeneous—or seek out sameness in a relationship to make it work. But from the point of view of self-actualization, I'm not convinced this is the answer. Because in the name of sameness, it may be neither one finds their unique expression in the world.

The true answer would have been in recognizing that each of us held a key for the other. Perhaps I needed to stop suppressing my newly-found yang side and allow it to come out–but in a more skillful, softer and more relaxed way. A yin with more of a yang balance. Perhaps Daren needed to stop swinging between needing to be the only decision maker, and then when questioned, taking offense and swinging to the yin side; totally withdrawing from any participation in an act of resistance. Maybe he needed to be comfortable leading as well as following. A yang with more of a yin balance.

LIFE TEACHES US BALANCE

Being on the land *had* taught me to find my yang side. It had taught me to move beyond so many self-imposed limitations and ideas about what I thought I could and couldn't do.

Once, when Daren was furious with me, he left me alone on the lower property while he, his son, and granddaughter stayed above. At first, I could feel myself collapsing into my old fears and insufficiencies. But I wiped my tears, stood up and went on. I could take care of myself. I had learned how to do this.

For the next several days, I lived completely on my own, splitting and hauling wood, carrying water, lighting the fire, tending it through the night, cooking for myself with the supplies available on hand. Even when the propane ran out I managed to cook for myself on the woodstove. Being completely alone at night scared me, especially as my supply of candles got low, but I would not give in. I cleaned the entire house from top to bottom. Then I pulled out supplies to fill holes in the cabin, and I began to stain the house.

I think Daren was surprised I did not drown in a puddle of my own tears five days later when he returned. Instead, I was up on top of a ladder staining the outside of the house looking quite surprised myself that he had decided to show up. In that moment I knew I had found an inner resolve. I had a glimpse of the person I could be, and I was proud to be. It had just taken being backed into a corner, with everything that mattered taken away from me, for me to discover it.

Glimpses are a gift. They are a view into another way of being we would never previously have imagined possible for ourselves. Though we may not yet have the capacity to act from that place over a sustained period of time, it does open up another window of possibility. With that possibility comes trust that, "I can act differently in the world than the way I have in the past." And with that trust, eventually comes momentum. What begins with seconds or minutes grows into hours, into days and can eventually become a way of life.

That's when I also began to see that my anger is related to empowerment and inner balance for an excess yin. If I didn't allow myself to get angry, if I was always nice, always sweet and always accommodating, I became weak and disempowered. When I used my anger, my defiance and my rebellion constructively, I could use it to become an upright, strong, forward-leaning woman in the world. Anger could bring a little yang into my life. I would have to circle a few more times around the barn until I really got that down though, because as soon as things went well outside, all thoughts of my inner fierceness would fall away. I would drop my willingness to stand up for myself. I would go back to being the little girl who would do anything to get the love she so desperately wanted.

Looking back, perhaps one of the things that kept us from finding the center point between us was my "edge" of living on the land. There was a marked difference in the way we related to each other when we were off the land; traveling, teaching, or working at the spa. We communicated more easily, had fun and were able to both share in common activities from a more equal place. In a certain way, it felt like we were in two relationships; the one on the land, and the one off the land.

MOVING

That winter, Daren decided he wanted us to be near his family on the East Coast of Canada, just outside Toronto. I was relieved and overjoyed. I thought this might be a new beginning.

We'd never really lived together with the comforts most people have, except on the road.

Returning home armed with some money from a workshop, we packed up our Jeep, in a snowstorm, and drove across the country. The Jeep developed an oil leak on the way. It would be too expensive to fix, so we stopped every hour or so to fill it up.

We made it this way, all the way across the country, and soon found an apartment I loved. We had just enough money for a deposit and first and last month's rent. It was toasty warm, with lots of light. A family friend had extra furniture in storage, which we gratefully accepted. We didn't have much work, but friends helped us get on our feet.

With the pressure and difficulties of the land off of my back, things began to go well for Daren and me. I got to know his family, and I enjoyed their company. We checked out the local churches, and learned Scottish dancing. I had a computer and phone at home and could run our business. Daren's priority was spending time with his family, so I was often alone. Now in a town, with my own work, I missed him, but didn't mind so much. Daren's brother had gifted us with a fitness club membership and we both went every day. This was a life I could manage.

As things got better between us, I became more comfortable and started to feel I could show more of who I was. I thought I could share my thoughts, and be an equal participant in our partnership. We even discussed this central issue between us. But it appeared Daren's view was still that, as the man, he should set the direction and make all the decisions. My job was to follow them. This was not meant as a power game. It was simply the way he had learned a man should behave in relationship. From his perspective, he was simply doing his best to fulfill his obligations. Confounded by this attitude and not knowing how to find my own voice in the midst of it, I gave up trying to convince him otherwise. But my need to have an equal say in our relationship choices did not go away.

One afternoon, I made a comment about our dwindling money and our job prospects. We had both been looking for steady work, with very few leads. A great opportunity arose for him as a personal trainer. He had worked with many movie stars and high-level executives in the past. The problem was he was overqualified. My problem was I had no permit for Canada, one of the reasons I went to the U.S. to work. Daren didn't want to take the job.

Feeling more open and confident, I told him I thought he should. We were spending too much money, and couldn't pay for next week's groceries, much less next month's rent. He immediately reacted, insisting I was telling him what to do, and no one was going to dictate his actions.

He stood up, said, "I won't be back for a long time," and left. Moments later he returned, only to say, "And I'm going back to the land."

My heart sank. I knew once he made a statement like that there was no going back. I tried to keep myself calm. We would talk and figure things out, I told myself. I was an adult now, and we could get through this if we both just said what we wanted and needed. We'd be able to find a middle ground, I thought.

Daren was gone all day and that night. When he returned, we didn't talk for the next few days. The pain in my back returned with a vengeance. The stress of his abrupt withdrawal upset my stomach. I could not hold down any food.

Finally, seeing how much I was suffering from the silent-treatment, he relented. I truly wanted to know what was so disturbing to him that he reacted that way. I may have been a bit directive in putting my opinion out there for fear of not having money to cover our bills, but I hadn't been stressed or reactive. I was simply stating facts. It didn't seem to warrant such an exaggerated response. I didn't know what was going on. So I asked.

"You always want to be in charge," he said. "You only think of yourself and what you want."

I took a breath and remained calm. I said nothing. I'd finally gotten him to talk to me, and now I wanted to hear it all.

"How do I do that?" I asked.

"You are trying to control me. You had us move here when I didn't really want to."

"I thought you wanted to be here to be with your family."

"Only for a month or two," he replied. "I didn't mean for us to stay here."

In all fairness, he was probably right. When Daren had mentioned wanting to go home to visit his family and spend significant time with them, I jumped on it like a fish starving for water. When he'd tried to backpedal on the time frame, I kept reminding him of his original plan like a dog with a bone. This was my chance to get out, and I was grabbing it with both hands.

He continued, "I want a woman who wants to be with me down by the river. Who wants to live on the land. All you want is to grow your business. Well, I've done it, and I can tell you it won't get you anywhere. After you have done it all you will see that it is all meaningless, and you will come back to me."

"Okay, well maybe I need time to figure that out for myself, just like you figured it out for yourself," I responded, trying to maintain a reasonable tone.

"What I've come to realize is that you are not the woman I hoped you would be. I'm with you now and I have to accept it."

There were two ways I could interpret what he'd just said: One, he accepted I did not fit his picture, but loved me anyway. Or two, he resented the fact he was stuck with me, someone who could never be what he wanted. Upon further probing, it turned out to be the latter.

No woman wants to hear that she is a disappointment, and I didn't want to be someone he'd settled for. I wanted to be with someone grateful for me, in spite of the disappointments.

It was at that moment I withdrew. I knew there was nothing further I could do.

Sometimes, as we move towards our center, the other cannot make the adjustment. A sudden change can cause the other person to feel threatened by the imminent perception of "loss of territory," especially when they are not sure they are ready to let go of it. As I began to find my own voice, I unintentionally triggered Daren's old fears about being dominated and told what to do. He saw me as the yang in the relationship; the one who always wanted to be in charge. This caused him to react with immediate resistance, trying to re-establish his sense of lost control by deciding to go back to the land.

Looking back for lessons, patience and timing would have helped. Thinking we were now in a good place and I could now voice my thoughts and opinions freely, I didn't take my time to move in carefully, slowly–with a little more yin. The right timing, the right situation and a gentle entry into the issue when we were both relaxed and open would have been skillful. I was stressed about money and I let that push me towards a hasty opinion rather than a well-conceived and gentle entry into an open-ended discussion.

This is why we often don't speak up, and instead settle for the status quo. We don't want to risk messing things up. But aren't things already *not* working? Or, maybe we don't want to face the pain of the others' inability to adjust to the transformation happening within us.

At times, many of us reach a point where it's better to try to shift relationship dynamics and fail, then not to try at all. For me, the pain it took to suppress who I was became so great (both emotionally and now physically), I felt I had no choice but to start being congruent with who I really was. In the process, I learned how to do it with greater skill by failing a few times.

At the very least, we are gathering information. Very important information that tells us if this relationship has the capacity to change to fit the transformation each individual in it is undergoing. If we can gather each little bit of information, just noting it, it will begin to create a very clear picture of the reality that lies before us. Sometimes a partner is ready to adjust, sometimes with time they will slowly come around, and sometimes they are just not ready. Sometimes the shoe is on the other foot and we are the ones who are not able to adjust, as I was not in my previous relationship.

The next day, Daren canceled our only workshop so we could return to B.C., but I knew this time I would not return. I decided to stay. I'd keep the apartment, work here, and run the workshop in his place. But when they called to confirm the details with me, Daren answered the phone. He was shocked. He insisted I was going back to B.C. with him, and that I would not be available to teach. I said nothing. I didn't dare. That option was closed.

CHAPTER TWENTY-FIVE

Y 35ᵀᴴ BIRTHDAY came and went. Daren and I had been together for three years. The pain in my back progressed to where I could only sleep for two or three hours most nights. The rest of the time I'd have to stand or walk to keep away the pain. Uninsured, I continued to go to the chiropractor, but got almost no relief. It didn't occur to me to get an MRI or x-ray. I just thought at some point the pain would go away.

I knew with increasing clarity there was no way I could go back to the land. The mere thought caused my gut and throat to tighten. My back was so bad I could barely function in an apartment with all the amenities. How could I possibly keep up with the demands there? I dreaded it.

Daren and I re-packed all the things we had brought with us. Probably knowing what was coming, but not willing to own up to it, I sent most of my things to my parents in Florida. Daren knew this. And we both knew we were coming to a parting of ways, but neither of us was truly willing to admit to it. At least I wasn't.

I wasn't sure what to do with myself. I knew I could not go back to the land. But I didn't want to run to my parents. I decided to go back to the place that still felt like home to me—Holland. My friends financed my trip home.

I arrived in Holland barely able to walk. Steve was shocked at my state. What had happened to me? I didn't know what was wrong. I thought being there would help, but the pain only seemed to intensify. I finally went to a physiotherapist who told me he thought I had a bulging disc. This was the first I had heard of anything like that. The trip, the pain, and the distance clarified things for me. I was ready to make myself a priority.

I had been trying to fit Daren's picture of a perfect mate. I had tried to make myself into something I couldn't be. The undesirable parts of me I simply suppressed, ignored or put away. Now my whole body, my whole being, was telling me, no more. My body simply could not carry any more. It couldn't carry the lifestyle, the piling debts, the constant lack of food, stability, and organization. And my spirit could no longer carry the weight of hiding who I was. I was against the wall and I had to make a decision. I could stay on the land and give up myself totally, or say "enough."

In the end, it was my body that forced my decision. I would like to say I came up with it on my own, but I didn't. Had my body not started to give out, I probably would have kept going. But part of me knew if I went back and kept living that life I would damage my body beyond repair. While I could barely walk now, there I might not be walking at all. I had to stand up for myself and for my body. If I didn't, no one else would or could. I left Holland virtually certain of my choice. But I didn't know if I'd have the guts to go through with it.

I left a message with a friend of Daren's confirming my return date to the land. It was now or never.

Due to a miscommunication, Daren was not at the airport to pick me up. In the past, I would have been nervous or fearful. But I had learned to maintain my center under greater challenges than this. As I was weighing my options, I recognized someone from the spa where we once worked, and asked if I could catch a ride. It would not get me home, but it would get me to town, within 90 minutes of the land. I would figure it out from there. From the spa, I got a ride to a colleague's house, and stayed overnight.

The next morning she drove me to the land. Daren was surprised to see me. He'd planned to pick me up the following day. Somehow our lines had gotten crossed. Determined not to take it personally, I settled in, but had to have an icepack on my back constantly to keep away the pain. As we all piled into the car to go to the hot springs the next day, I could barely sit.

Things were getting worse. Whether true or not, I felt my back was telling me to make this move. And realistically, there was no way I could survive on the land in this kind of pain. I had to get to a place where I could rest my back and have regular access to medical treatment. The life out here was so irregular and difficult, our finances so uncertain, I would not be able to get the kind of care, or pay for the kind of recovery I needed. I could barely even get up and down the hill to our cabin.

A day or two later I knew the time had come. I waited for hours at the cabin until Daren returned home. We had been living alongside one another rather than with one another for some time now and I didn't know when to expect him home.

"I need to talk," I said. We took a few moments to get ourselves situated on the porch.

"I need to live a life where I am happy. I need to be free to teach, to do what I love to do, to be the person that I am. I can't be the person you want me to be. I still love you, but I can't be that person. It is time for me to let go and move on."

At first he didn't quite get what I was saying. He began a sentence and then broke off abruptly in realization. "You want to break up," he said, his voice heavy with regret.

Neither of us said anything. I could feel the resignation in his tone. We both had so much invested in making a relationship work. But the truth was we were both miserable, and neither of us was getting what we really needed.

"I need to be free," I finally said. "I can't do this anymore."

To express those words was a monumental step for me. I have always been the yin person who could be flexible, who could accommodate, who would do anything, even compromise her own boundaries so other people would be happy. I never wanted to confront, say no, or risk being not liked. Now I was taking a stand. I felt shaky doing it, but I knew for my own well-being I had no other choice. Life had finally pushed me to such an extreme that I was pushing back. I was saying "Enough!" I was choosing a "me" I had only seen in brief glimpses; a powerful woman, finding her own self-expression in the world.

This was not the first time the possibility of breaking up had come up. The last time Daren had brought it up, I played cheerleader and said we could make it through. I wanted to believe it was true, but even then I knew it wasn't. Now, I knew Daren had called it right the first time; I had been the one deceiving myself.

He moved a few of his things out of the cabin, and would stay the night in the trailer above. He said he'd be making dinner for us, his son, and his granddaughter, so I said I'd come up and help in a little while.

As I watched Daren walk up the hill alone, I watched the fairytale that had been crumbling over time, finally fall to dust. It was done. I felt sad. I still loved him. I also felt as if a great weight was lifted. I was *finally* free...free of wanting, needing and hoping for a time when everything would work out. I was free from trying to wrestle with this life and turn myself into someone more desirable. It was what it was. I was what I was. The two didn't fit. That was it. I finally found the guts to make the call–to admit the fantasy I had been holding on to for so many years was just that. There was regret, but at least I would not spend the rest of my life trying to be something I would never be happy being. I was free to be myself. The question was, would I really be able to do it, or were there still more lessons to learn?

About forty-five minutes later I painstakingly made my way up the hill. Daren and I worked side-by-side preparing the meal, as we had done so many times before. Now the harmony with which we worked seemed even more profound, yet out of place, in the context of our impending breakup.

At dinner he made the announcement. He was very cool and matter-of-fact when he told everyone I would be going away. He didn't say it would be for good, and I didn't see the point in hammering on the fact.

My step-granddaughter was very sweet. She said she didn't want me to go. She would miss me. I would miss her, too. Though she was only nine years old, she was an old soul. In many ways I'd provided stability in her life, but she'd also provided the same in mine. I regretted leaving her and hoped she knew how much I loved her. She was the only granddaughter I'd ever had. She'd loved the effect she had every time she called me "Grandma" in front of people. She was blonde. I was dark. I was only 35. When people did a double-take she would giggle. That night she gave me her favorite little butterfly ring and told me not to forget her. Touched to my core I promised I wouldn't and hugged her close.

That night was my last on the land. I tried to commit it all to memory. So much had happened here. So much suffering, yet so many breakthroughs, so many joyous moments with a quality of magic I would never again experience. Though it was time to move on, I was grateful for this experience. I was grateful for everything I had learned and become through it. Everything that had come before had brought me to this point—the point where I finally chose myself.

The next morning, Daren came down to help me carry my luggage up the hill. His son and granddaughter were asleep in the trailer above. I did not awaken the little one, but gently shook Daren's son awake. Though we were never openly in conflict with one another, in my own world of pain and angst, I had at times judged him harshly against my own code of responsibility. And, against my own will I had sometimes felt him as an obstruction between Daren and myself. I'm sure he had felt it, though neither of us had ever exchanged words.

As he woke I whispered, looking straight into his eyes, "I want to tell you something. I went through a really hard time here. I was in a lot of pain, and because of that I judged you unfairly. Will you please forgive me?"

He nodded his head just once, his eyes softening. He was a good soul. He understood. We hugged each other. I knew any unfinished business between us was complete.

Daren and I walked slowly to the car and began the long drive to the airport. We didn't say much. Here and there one of us would ask the other about something, needing clarification, trying to put the puzzle pieces in place. All things considered, the silence was comfortable. We'd simply come to the end of the road. It was a fact. Not something to be upset about.

We approached the Spokane airport. Daren pulled the car up to the departure terminal. He got out of the Jeep, pulled out my suitcases and put them on a cart near the curb. Then he turned to me. He took me in his arms and hugged me. Purposefully he kissed me on the lips.

Looking straight into my eyes he said, "Fly high, honey. Don't let anything stop you."

Without another word he got back into the Jeep, pulled out into traffic and drove away.

I could feel the sobs building in my throat but I pushed them down. He had gotten it after all. He understood what this was all about for me.

CHAPTER TWENTY-SIX

AFTER CANADA, I first landed at the house of some very good friends who took me in and took care of me as my back began to heal. It was a long and arduous process. But it was not only my body that was healing; it was my psyche. Unable to walk more than a few steps or carry more than a few ounces, I spent much time alone, taking baths, watching reruns of 'Will and Grace." I needed time to dial down from the extreme stress my emotions had been under for so long.

Time and contemplative silence brought forth insight. I came to see things with greater perspective. I began to see the perfection of things just as they had been, and I came to an internal sense of peace. I resumed teaching, even in my compromised physical state.

It was actually in this state of limited physical capability that I learned to truly practice yoga. I had no choice but to be completely present and unattached to getting anywhere. If I tried to be other than where I was, if I tried to force my body, I would pay for it with hours, and sometimes days, of pain. I learned to become acutely sensitive and attentive to the body's intelligence over the voice of my ego, which so desperately wanted to show up as the strong, powerful teacher who could do everything. But it wasn't so. By accepting reality, I learned the true meaning of yoga—being at peace with how things are. With time, and listening to my body, it regained most of its former capabilities.

During this time of reflection and healing I began to see a pattern. From the very first time we met, Daren had shown me how to express the part of me that was deeply buried inside. I was a teenage girl, confined by a world of watchful eyes. Suddenly he came into my life, and through dance he showed me a part of myself I had never known existed. It was the first time I experienced spirit as it uniquely flowed through me, through this personality, through this body and this mind. He had been the agent of that first glimpse.

Many years later, the life we had became the vehicle through which I finally broke through my own limitations to come back to that self. In yoga and dance he'd taught me to do things I never thought my body could do. I learned to trust my body in a way I never had before. During my time on the land, I'd shattered my own concepts about what I needed to survive. I'd learned to succeed in an environment that would have gotten to the best of "a lesser version" of me. And finally, I learned to say, "This is not me."

Sometimes the only way we can know who we truly are, is by fully experiencing who we are *not*. Sometimes we have to be pushed far beyond our edge, we have to suffer before we will finally draw the line. I felt that now my line had been drawn. Though I might backslide at times, I knew who I was. I knew what my life was about. I would not allow anything to take me off course. But it had taken my being pushed to one extreme for me to stand firm in my own essence. Now, in a way I never could have imagined, Daren had again become the catalyst towards my own self-actualization.

Maybe destiny is not always the happy ending we think it implies. Maybe destiny is the perfect confluence of events brought together so we can learn the lessons we need to learn. I believe it *was* destiny that brought us together. I just mistook what that destiny was. It wasn't the fairytale ending. It was me finally coming into my own as a woman, with something to contribute to the world in my own right. I believe, on a level Daren himself wasn't even aware of, he played his part perfectly. The relationship, the land, the circumstances did their respective jobs. That was the destiny. And the destiny fulfilled itself.

Sometime later as these realizations began to crystallize, I wrote Daren a letter:

My Dear Daren,

I'm writing you to share my thoughts and feelings around us and our relationship. First of all, I want you to know that I love you, and always will. There is nothing that could ever change that, from the very moment I first met you. As I reflect upon the time we had together, there are so many things that come to mind that make me smile with appreciation of who you are, what you taught me, and the wonderful time we had together—a time I wouldn't trade for anything. I remember magical nights on the land, our home filled with candlelight, making love, dancing around in our living room and cooking dinner. I treasure that time and those memories.

I get that your life needs to be about your in-depth studies, your freedom to be in nature, to garden and support the upbringing of your family. And you've earned it. You have put in your time, and now this is your time for inner reflection.

For me, I'm just coming into my own as the full expression of me. My life is about realizing the truth of who I am, and helping others do the same. For me, this takes the form of teaching. To do anything else, even in the name of the love I feel for you, would not feel complete.

What I would like more than anything is to create a form for us that is appropriate to what we can really provide each other. I'd love to be able to talk with you on the phone and have us be able to share what we're up to and offer a listening ear to each other. But I understand if that doesn't work for you.

From a karmic perspective I feel the perfection of us. From the very first time I met you, you freed me. It was in the dance with you that I first experienced myself unbounded. Now, I feel that all we've gone through together has brought me to the place where I am ready to live from that place of full self-expression. I am grateful you have been the one through whom I found freedom.

I love you,
Kamini

In the end I went to Canada to complete things. I had no idea how it would be. Would he be angry? Resentful? Neutral? Distant? Daren was working at the spa, so I would meet him there. As I walked through those doors, as I had so many times before, it was like walking back in time. I looked for his face, and then heard his voice. That same deep, resonant voice I had known for so long. I walked downstairs and into the dining room. He was talking with a client, looked up, and saw me. Immediately he came towards me and we embraced. The old joy to see one another was still there, though this time more mature, more subdued.

With cups of tea in our hands, we sat. Much time had passed since we had seen one another. The initial reactions and resentments that once seemed so real to us had faded with time. In its place had come insight, learning about ourselves, and understanding of one another. Each of us was eager to share what we had learned. We talked about the mistakes each of us had made. We accepted each other in our humanness.

My fairytale about Daren was it was our destiny to be together. As such, I believed my life would be "filled full" by Daren. He would be my savior. I was so blinded by my own idea of him I never actually took the time to find out who he really was, and what he wanted and needed at this point in his life. It never occurred to me to make a choice that would include prioritizing my own well-being and self-expression in the world. I felt if he was going to fill me, then I didn't need to fill myself up. I could leave it up to him. However, no one can fulfill us indefinitely, and Daren was no exception. My hope, expectation and dependency was built up so high, he could never have fulfilled it all.

Had I really looked at the facts, I would have seen the life he so loved had me so far out over my edge I could barely function. I stopped attending to my own happiness and fulfillment to be with him. In doing so, I left behind the aspect I most needed to bring to the relationship—me. I thought it was the "romantic" thing to do. Now looking back I cannot think what in the world would be romantic or even logical about abandoning the person

Daren loved, for a facsimile of her, and then believing a true relationship between two souls could occur.

I thought I was loving Daren by playing into his fantasy of love. Probably the most loving thing I could have done was show him very clearly, honestly and directly who I was and what I really wanted in my life as soon as I realized how different we were.

But that would have required a total willingness to let go of what I had so desperately craved for so many years. It would have required a level of self-love that was confident in its own ability to be happy with or without this relationship. Though my mind knew differently, my actions reflected a deeper conviction that the only avenue to love was through another. I believed I couldn't do without that love. I couldn't risk it. So instead I played along.

BUILDING OUR ENERGY RESERVE SUPPORTS WHOLENESS

Daren and I were both convinced if we could just change something about the other, everything would be okay. In the end, we realized if each of us had been living our best, fullest, most self-expressed lives, we would not have been focused on the other as our source happiness, and found the possibility for our own.

Our first and most important job in a loving relationship is to do, be, and act in a way that supports our own wholeness. We do this by attending to our own energy reserve so we are not bringing an empty cup to the relationship and waiting for the other to fill it.

When we are filled full by life—self-expressed, energized, vital, balanced, inspired; it naturally spills over to the ones around us. Our heart is naturally open when it is overflowing—our cup runneth over and love is showered on the person or people we've chosen to shower it on.

This changes the game from, "What am I missing and how can you fill it?" to "Who am I and how can I give it to you?" When we do this, it naturally brings wholeness to the relationship.

On the other hand, the times when we are most empty and needy are when things tend to go wrong in relationship. We become dependent on what the other person says or does, and when they don't meet the expectations we are relying on to fill our empty cup, we take it personally and react. Sometimes we try to control. Or we get into a push/pull where one needs alone time and the other is needy.

We can affect this tendency by making sure we feel good in ourselves. We can make sure the internal fuel is already there and our energy field is strong. Then we have much greater "cushion" to handle any disappointments or frustrations. Our cushion, or energy field, has four primary elements that can add or detract from it: physical, mental, emotional and spiritual. We need to attend to the energy of the physical body through things like diet and exercise. But we also need to attend to our mental and emotional energy by being congruent with it. We can do that by balancing yin and yang. That means saying no when we need to, and setting boundaries *before* we get pushed too far. It means taking time to feel sad, or express something that just needs to be said. When we do this on an ongoing basis (before things come to a head), we create a clear, open channel for the flow of life energy. That is our fuel. And that is what keeps us balanced, alive and vital. It keeps us fully rooted in ourselves. That doesn't mean we have to deal with things right on the spot, but when the time is right, we make the effort to bring things back into inner alignment.

From this place, we are more able to allow irritations to roll off our back. We are much less likely to get into a fight. There is much less need to control if we know we don't have to control someone else to feel good. We can just feel good. This happens when both partners are connected and interdependent, yet rooted in their own being.

That's why the best thing we can do when we are getting upset is to change our internal state. And I'm not talking about a pint of Ben and Jerry's or a drink. That is medicating. I'm talking about rebalancing and refilling the fuel tank. This could look like going to the gym, taking a walk, sitting quietly in nature, read inspiring teachings or reflecting on ourselves. These things can bring us back to our center so the need for Ben and Jerry's is no longer there. After returning to a greater sense of completeness, we may still need to come back and work things out, but they will tend to come from a more even-keeled, less reactive place.

Our second most important job is to support our partner in maintaining *their* sense of wholeness. Compatibility lies in our ability to be able to support what our partner does, and they to support what we do, whether we like it or not. If what they need to feel whole impinges on our well-being, or puts us on our edge in some way, then we need to determine how much of that edge we can relax with before we go too far over into toleration mode. Chances are, if we are living our own best life, we will have more capacity to relax with what our partner needs. If we are not, we will tend to resent it and it will be more difficult.

The other thing we need to recognize is no one person will be able to meet us on all levels. There are six major areas where we seek connection with others: physical affection, mental affinity, emotional connection, spiritual awareness, sexual satisfaction, and social interaction. It is our job to recognize that some of these connections will happen through a primary intimate relationship. Others will not. Instead of blaming the other for their shortcomings, we can create our own experience of wholeness by nurturing these connections with others—of course within our commitment to our primary relationship.

COMMITTED RELATIONSHIP IS A SUBSET OF LOVE

Loving someone and being in a committed relationship are two different things. Love is a beautiful, powerful, experience of heart opening. But it would be a mistake to assume that because we experience powerful opening of our own heart in the presence of another, they are the person we should commit to being with in a relationship. In theory, we could open our heart to anyone and experience love. But that doesn't mean we would have a relationship with them.

Moving from an intense, open-hearted connection to the form of a relationship requires another set of lenses and close examination, beginning with compatibility in the six areas previously described. It is a very specific and finite subset that includes but is not limited to the experience of heart opening. Too often, when we assume ourselves to be empty, pretty much anyone who fits the general blueprint looks like they can fill us up. This common pattern is what keeps us from choosing a partner who can truly be an asset and a companion on the journey in daily aspects of life as well as the emotional and spiritual ones.

As we mature, we tend to have much greater clarity on what it is that creates wholeness and completeness in us. In general, there is much greater priority put on preserving this and less willingness to throw it all away when a potential mate comes along. We begin to look and see if a potential partner will be able to add to a baseline of wholeness that has already been established.

The pitfall of course is this in itself can become a rigid structure. We may become so stuck in our own individualized way of doing things and fearful of losing ourselves that we will only allow another person in if they play the game by our rules. If they do not, they are promptly shown the door. This may keep us empowered in one arena, but does not teach us to bring that empowerment to a relationship. Mastery is not a place to stop, it is a place to practice expanding that mastery to more and more arenas. This means, by definition, there will be failures along the way.

LOVE LESSONS

Many of us have heard this stuff all our lives. It all sounds really good, and maybe we've even been able to articulate it to others. But that doesn't necessarily mean the lesson has been truly digested and assimilated. That is the purpose of life experience and the lessons we are here to learn. Sometimes there is no other way to get a lesson than to live it. Someone might tell us all about swimming. We might absorb it all. It might make great sense to us. We might even be able to repeat it to others and teach them about swimming. But until we actually *experience* swimming, it is not real. There is no depth to the wisdom. It might be accurate, but has not been lived. It is the living that makes the difference. It is what adds depth and understanding to those very same words.

Many times we might judge ourselves for having to "learn the hard way." Why couldn't we have just heard all the right stuff and been done with it? Perhaps for some of the most crucial lessons of our lives there is no other way than the "hard way." It has to be *lived*. We have to know the lesson to the very core of our being, not just as a concept, but also as an experiential knowing.

Through experience things become a part of who we are and the way we naturally look at the world, not just a viewpoint we artificially adopt as we desperately try to do the "right" thing. Then our choices are not about "willpower" and "doing what I should do." We make those same choices simply because we know through experience the other way simply doesn't work. Then it's not about "good" decisions or "bad" decisions or "right" or "wrong." It's about understanding what works in the context of living a fully-expressed "personal best" life. Our choices either serve that purpose or they don't. They are not right or wrong in terms of what other people say.

"So why, then, are you writing this book?" you might ask.

Most of us, with the biggest lessons in our lives, tend to learn cyclically. We will encounter a lesson one time around and will not quite get it. We may go around again, this time having learned a few things and gained a little bit of skill. We may notice we are doing it, but may still feel bound to make the same choice anyway. It is not until we begin to recognize what we are doing is truly not working and is causing us suffering that we begin to be willing to break out of the cyclical pattern.

Life itself will do this for us each time we go around, because we are not just going around, we are going up. Like a spiral staircase. Each time, it seems like we are back at the same place we began, but not quite. If we are willing to look, we have the opportunity to see the same situation from a greater height, a little more clearly, with more objectivity and perspective. It is this perspective that provides us the opportunity to break the cycle and get out. Until we see clearly what we are doing, and acknowledge the connection between what we are doing and the pain we are experiencing, we will keep doing it.

Similarly, my aim in sharing this story and these insights is not to prevent the very natural life lessons each and every one of us must experience, but hopefully to provide a perspective— perhaps a previously unseen connection that allows insight into the choices we are making and the outcomes we are getting. If we can see what we are doing, it may be just the push we need to break that cycle and get off the merry-go-round. But even if we don't, it's okay. In the timeless words of author Ilanya van Sant, "You're not ready 'til you're ready."

Even when we break the cycle, vestiges remain. Old habits and ways of thinking will still come up. But the less we feed them, the less power they will have over us until they begin to fade, each time exerting less and less influence over our choices.

Now armed with these insights, Daren and I understood it was time to go back to our lives and begin the work of becoming who we were meant to be. Not as defined by society, or a partner, or even a concept we had picked up. We had been very crucial to each other in defining who we were meant to be in the world. Now we had to follow through.

CHAPTER TWENTY-SEVEN

S INCE LEAVING the large yoga center he had founded, my father had taken some time for himself and my mother. Having first moved to Pennsylvania, my brother, father and mother had now started a small retreat center housing up to 40 people on a spring-fed lake in the lush greenery of central Florida. My mother and father loved their new home. It reminded them of their beloved India. The simpler lifestyle appealed to them both. The setup was similar to what they had once had when they had set up their first retreat all those years ago. The teacher trainings I had been involved with had been moved to the Florida location. Now I was single and had no place to go, I could feel the family strings pulling me there.

Until now I had spent my life trying to avoid the elephant in the room. That elephant was my father, and also my life purpose. I had always known I would follow in my father's footsteps in some way. I had known it as a child. I had known it when I went to college and decided I wanted nothing to do with spiritual stuff. Since my twenties, I had always found ways to keep my distance—literally. I'd lived thousands of miles away in Holland, and then made myself virtually impossible to reach in Canada. By avoiding my dad, I was also avoiding the immensity of what I felt my life was about. It was too scary to face. I felt it was egotistical for me to put myself forward this way. I wasn't perfect enough to teach, I told myself. But the course of my life brought me back over and over to teaching, each time with increasing force and certainty.

Now I knew I could not do anything but that. I could no longer deny it. It was through teaching that I stepped out of my small, confined self. My heart opened. Fear dissolved. Clarity and wisdom came through from a place beyond my small personality. I was following in my father's footsteps, but I had come upon it in my own unique way.

But just how much was I supposed to follow? Completely? A little bit? Not at all? I didn't know, and it was hard for me to tell.

Though not necessarily spoken out loud, my father's wish had always been that I would carry on his work. I had spent my entire life trying to keep my father at bay in an effort to discover who I was, independent of his far-reaching personality. I had gotten used to pushing away anything he wanted me to do, so I couldn't tell if my aversion to his wish was reactionary or intuitive.

There was also the issue of feeling I had to please my father by doing what he wanted. Instead of creating a clear boundary and saying, "This is all I want to do, that is all," I put obstructions between my father's wish and myself. I did not want to risk losing his love by disappointing him outright, so I created some very good excuses instead.

But the truth was, I wasn't just avoiding my father's wishes, I was also avoiding stepping into my own greater potential. It was easier for me to be small and insignificant than to step up and fully own what I wanted to do with my life, to dedicate myself to it completely. That would require hard work. It would require commitment. But most of all it would require my believing in myself. This quote by Marianne Williamson captures the feeling perfectly.

Our deepest fear is not that we are inadequate.
Our deepest fear is that we are powerful beyond measure.
It is our light, not our darkness that most frightens us.

We ask ourselves, who am I to be brilliant, gorgeous, talented and fabulous?
Actually, who are you not to be?
You are a child of God. Your playing small doesn't serve the world.

There's nothing enlightened about shrinking so that other people won't feel insecure around you.
We were born to make manifest the glory of God that is within us. It's not just in some of us; it's in everyone.

And, as we let our own light shine, we unconsciously give other people permission to do the same. As we are liberated from our own fear, our presence automatically liberates others.

Now I felt my time had come. It was time for me to allow myself to shine, to stop playing small. I was going to say yes to my father's wishes and see what happened.

I could have resisted as I had done so many times before. I had defined large portions of my life trying to get away from what I thought my father wanted from me. But to the degree that my life choices were in reaction to him, was the degree to which I was still living at his effect. Unless I faced this, I would be living in reaction to my dad, whether I was in Florida or not.

Now I was being asked to come back to face what I hadn't faced in the past. I wasn't really even sure what it was, but I knew it was calling my name.

I moved to the nearest city, about a 40-minute drive from the new yoga retreat in Florida, and found an apartment I loved in an old Victorian home. It had huge rooms with wood floors and high ceilings. Eventually, the drive got to be too much, and I moved within a few miles.

I soon settled into a routine of overseeing the marketing and logistics of the programs at the retreat, as well as directing many of them. The idea was that my brother and I would run things. Eventually I would not only be the program director, but would also be my father's successor in the spiritual lineage he had come from. I did not know if I was ready for this. This was what I had been trying to avoid all my life.

The thought of carrying on the lineage scared me, but I didn't know if that was because it was something I needed to step into, but hadn't yet found the courage, or if it was because it was simply not right for me.

I pushed my misgivings aside and began working long hours on administration, finding myself thinking about details until the early hours of the morning. Teaching began to take a back seat to my administrative duties, which were many, and weighed heavily upon my shoulders.

Though I could administrate and run a center, it was clearly not my passion. What really lit me up was teaching. The one thing stopping me from speaking the truth and simply moving on was the fear of disappointing my father.

As a young girl, I had decided the only way I could secure my father's love was by being the daughter he wanted. That was where I had learned my elemental yin pattern. Now, he was asking me to carry on the one thing he lived for–the teachings of his lineage. He was asking me to maintain a center he had put so much time and effort into, thinking one day I would take over. How in the world could I tell him I didn't want it? How could I tell him what he wanted to give me didn't feel like a gift at all, but rather, a burden? It was like throwing a gift, one he had lovingly created his whole life to give to me, back in his face. So, in my yin way, I continued on. I kept working, kept teaching, and kept hoping that some outside force would come and take me out of this situation. I hoped maybe someone else would want to come in and run the center. I hoped I would be off the hook and would not have to confront my father.

We do so much not to have to disappoint the ones we love. We do so much so that we won't have to risk confronting someone with something they don't want to hear. But in the process we compromise ourselves. We put ourselves in a holding pattern hoping for something to save us, when all we have to do is tell the truth. But that is the last thing we want to do. We'd rather suffer than cause someone else pain or risk losing their love. Instead, we take the burden ourselves, sometimes for years, so we won't have to step up and say what we really want.

The yin pattern I had developed with my father from a young age had become so second nature to me, at first I didn't even realize why I was doing what I was doing. I convinced myself this was what I really wanted. As I became more aware of the inner discord arising inside of me, the option of telling my father was not even on the table. It hadn't been eliminated as a possibility, it simply never occurred to me as being one.

This is how we develop limitations in many aspects of our lives. We learn a certain way of being, usually to secure love or approval, and then repeat it over and over. Even when that behavior becomes a constraint, we continue to repeat it because it seems there is no option but to keep behaving that way.

In order to break the cycle, I would have to be willing to break a deep-seated pattern—my yin-based need to please. This pattern didn't just show up with my dad, it showed up in most other aspects of my life. But if I could do it here, where it was most challenging and closest to the core, I would see I could do it anywhere.

My teaching, however, continued to develop. I found a personal teaching style and voice, which felt like an authentic reflection of me. I enjoyed bringing in stories from my personal life to show how the principles of yoga applied to everyday life. I wanted to make the teaching fun, enjoyable, and relatable—something we could all laugh with as we learned. I felt my strength came from my willingness to be imperfect, to show how we can all be just as we are and still be fully-empowered human beings.

In the midst of this, my mother, who had had cancer many years before, was facing more frequent bouts of illness. She needed my care and attention, and I wanted to give it to her.

Her tests had shown she was in liver failure as a result of a bad blood transfusion from cancer surgery years before, and did not have long to live. When my mother heard it, she was not shocked. She was not upset. She was ready, she said. I told her I would support her in any choice she made.

When my mother first had cancer, I was seventeen years old. I was so scared of losing her and uncomfortable with illness, I was not able to be there for her in the way I could have been. I had always felt bad about that. This was my chance to make it right.

The only thing I had to give my mother now was me. Her fear was that she would die alone. I told her I would not leave her side. I promised her I would be with her to the end and she would not be alone.

As my mother's condition progressively worsened, the daughter became the mother. Along with a nurse, my mom's best friend, and my aunt, we took care of her at home. We attended to her medications, her food, her bathing and personal care as she became more and more like a child. My father and brother would come and massage her feet and chant to her each morning and night. Every time my father would walk into the room her face would light up and she would open her arms wide to take him in her arms.

In preparation for her end she had organized her room before she had gotten too ill. She had decided what should go to whom, what she would wear for her cremation, and even the details of her funeral. Even in her death, she wanted to keep the burden of her passing as light as possible.

I slept on the floor next to my mother every night. During the day I would go home for two hours, change my clothes and come back while the nurse cared for her in my absence. My mother became my life. As she became less and less able to do things, she allowed herself to surrender and trust me. Though it was painful to know my mother was leaving, I experienced a sense of fulfillment more powerful than anything I had ever known. I'd had a glimpse of it in my teaching, but it was nothing like this. I realized that in the depth of my total and one-pointed devotion to her, I was released from my own personal drama.

I felt whole. I felt I was serving in a way I was meant to serve. And in that total devotional focus there was no room for doubt, for second-guessing. There was just giving to something greater than myself. And in doing so I was finding myself.

My mother passed away while my father, my brother and I were by her side. But in her passing, she had given me a gift. My mother had always radiated love and compassion. She devoted herself totally to her faith and to her life. She gave herself to serving others with no resistance or doubt. She just did it with no expectation of return. In her dying, I learned what that meant. I understood how true service could be a powerful tool in finding my own sense of wholeness.

The question now was, where and how was I meant to serve? And, on another level, whom would I serve? My own path? Or the vision my father had for me? My pattern was leading me to serve my father's hopes and wishes for me—in the same way I had tried to serve Daren's hopes and wishes. But it was chafing at me. I was no longer willing to be reigned-in by *any form* that didn't completely reflect who I was.

From the outside looking in, anyone would have told me I had the opportunity of a lifetime. I wanted to teach. I wanted to serve. Well, here was a place I could do both with ease. Everything was set up for me. A facility was here, a following, a structure, a system of teachings. All my father had to do was declare me the successor and it would all be mine. I would have a vehicle to share myself in the world. Since I was now clear this was what my life was about, there shouldn't be a problem—right? All I had to do was say yes. But it didn't feel right.

Growing up, I had seen what it was like to be a Guru. Everyone expecting the Guru to be perfect and unassailable. If I was in that position I would feel I had to live up to the picture of what a Guru "should" be. I would not be able to go out dancing, or have a Martini with my friends. I would not be able to go to the movies or talk about cute men. I would have to comport myself in a manner befitting a Guru, and that just wasn't me. I had spent a lifetime learning how to be my full self, but now I'd have to go back to living up to a picture of spiritual teacher. To me, it felt like golden chains. I might have everything I wanted, but I would be chained, nonetheless.

I went around and around in my mind, trying to come up with scenarios where I could take on the lineage and still be myself. But everything felt like a half-hearted compromise. I had come into this life to be me. And this was not me.

My father had done the same thing himself. He'd had to find a form that allowed him to most powerfully transmit his teachings and the powerful energetic experience that came with it. And that was very different from the way *his* teacher had done it. My father's teacher, Bapuji, had been a monk. My father was a householder with children. Bapuji had meditated 10 hours a day. My father's practice was primarily oriented to serving others' evolution through teaching. My father had found a way that had worked for him. Now I had to find the courage to do the same thing even though it would mean his dream scenario was not going to happen.

To some degree, in a different setting, I had gone around the circle again. But this time I had caught on a little more quickly. This time, instead of putting myself into a position where I committed to living up to someone else's picture of me, I was going to tell the truth. That was the most loving thing I could do for everyone concerned, rather than promising something I could never wholeheartedly deliver.

My father would be disappointed in the short term. But it was not my job to keep my father from being disappointed. My father had been disappointed lots of times, and he had gotten over it. I couldn't protect him from pain–and I couldn't compromise my own well-being in order to try. My job was to be a fully actualized human being in this world. I would tell the truth as skillfully as I could, but I had to be willing to risk the separation that might happen between us. I had to trust that even if I didn't live up to my father's dream for me, in the end he would love me anyway. And if he didn't, I would have to accept it because my first job was to love and care for myself.

This was a huge leap of faith for me. I was breaking from my old patterns in a way I had never dared to consider. Now I was doing it in the biggest way possible. I was forging an unknown path no one, least of all me, expected. I was letting go of a secure and certain future for an unseen possibility. I didn't know where it would take me, but I was willing to find out.

That same day, I went over to see my father. As he came down the stairs he said my energy felt very different, very open. In the same way I had done with Daren, I had tried to please my father on the outside, but my inner resistance to fulfilling his wishes kept me pushing him away, even resenting him, energetically. And of course he felt it. Now that I was clear, I had no need to push my father away. There was no need for resentment now because I was ready to live a life that reflected me.

As we sat down, I could feel the words I had needed to say all these years at the back of my throat. It was now or never.

I took a breath in and leapt into the void. "Dad," I began, "I've always felt that in order for you to love me I had to do what you wanted. I was afraid that if I didn't, you wouldn't love me. All these years I've been trying to please you. But I resented it at the same time. That's why you've always felt me pushing you away when you wanted to be close."

"I know what you really want is for me to be happy. I tried my best to be happy here, doing this. I put everything I had into it. But I'm realizing this is just not me. I don't want a yoga center. You enjoy the community it brings, and the feeling of common purpose. To me it just feels like a burden."

"I know for you this center is the perfect vehicle. But I have to do it differently–just like you had to do it differently from the way Bapuji did. I feel in my heart I will always carry the lineage no matter what, whether I have an official title or not. But I can't fit into the role of a Guru. I feel it would take away from what I have to offer instead of adding to it. The role of Guru empowers *you*, but it would chain *me*. I tried to do it because I wanted you to be happy. I wanted you to have what you wanted. But it wouldn't make me happy. I would feel stuck, and I wouldn't be happy, and I know that can't be what you want for me."

My dad's eyes began to tear up and he said, "I'm so happy to hear you talking to me like this. This is what I've wanted for so long." He took me in his arms and I started to cry.

"I love you, my baby," he said, his voice breaking from the tears as he wiped my face. "I just want to be your friend. I want to guide you and help you if you will let me. You don't have to be here if you don't want to be. I want you to be happy. I want you to do what you love. But keep talking to me. Let me help you. Let me guide you. I've learned a lot, and I can show you how things work. I just want us to stay connected."

I nodded my head, unable to speak. My throat choked up with tears.

He continued on, "But I will tell you what I want, too. That doesn't mean you have to do it. I have to state my preferences too, and if that doesn't happen I will let go."

With all the scenarios I had imagined, I had never imagined this one. All this time I'd been holding back who I was so I could be what my dad wanted. And all along what he'd really wanted was a real relationship, with the real me. Since my teenage years, I'd never let him close. I'd learned to hide myself away thinking the true me would not be loved. We'd never truly connected because I'd never shared myself. Now that I was sharing myself, even in a way that could have been devastating, he was happy. We'd found each other again.

And that first tenuous connection would continue to grow. I had a father. A real dad in a way that I'd never felt before. And it wasn't because he was any different, but because I had been willing to let down my guard and let him see me.

I'd finally broken the chains of my old habits. I'd finally let speaking the truth take precedence over my need to be loved. I'd stopped trying to live up to another person's picture. Now my slate was clean. I could craft a life that was an authentic, wholehearted reflection of me. It was the beginning of a new life. My life.

CHAPTER TWENTY-EIGHT

S HORTLY AFTER, I stepped down from my administrative
position at the yoga center, but would continue to lead
the key training programs. I decided to move to Phoenix,
Arizona where my best friend lived, and set up a new life. Steve
flew over from Holland to make the trip and help me move.

Driving down the highway, my past moving further and
further away with each mile, I could sense an enormous burden
draining away, new energy beginning to buoy up through my
body. I felt my spirit coming alive, freedom surging through my
veins. By degrees, I began to see I could do anything I chose.
My life had only been limited by the constraints I had put on it.

WE HAVE NEVER BEEN LIMITED EXCEPT IN OUR OWN PERCEPTION

I once read a story about the training of young baby elephants
in India. The Mahout (or elephant trainer) would attach the
young elephant by chain to a nearby tree until it learned it could
not move more than a few feet when tethered. Even when the
elephant had grown into an adult and could easily break free of
a tree of any size, it would not. It had learned to live within the
limits of its universe, not recognizing its own capacity to break
free of an assumed reality. Even when chained but not secured
to anything, it would not move more than a few feet. The elephant was no longer limited by external factors, but was still
living as if it were.

In a certain way, I felt like that elephant. I'd accumulated
assumed limitations which shackled me to the illusion of a nar-
rowly confined life--not recognizing the chains were powerless
except in my own mind. I had the power to break free all along.

Now that I was no longer chained by my need for others'
approval, I was free to create my life in any way I wanted. Until
now, so much of my life had been fettered by others' opinions

and ideas of who I should be, or my need to please the ever-neb-
ulous "them." Now I could see I had never been limited except
in my own perception.

This dawning freedom came in stages as the past still called.
For a little while, things between my father and I were a little
strained as he adjusted, but with time that began to ease. In the
beginning, I felt guilty. I still felt I'd abandoned my brother and
let my father down. But even with that feeling, there was no way
I was going back. It was not worth giving up my life just to avoid
feeling bad for a little while. My leaving had created a space, and
life would fill that vacuum. That's the way things always work.
Something else always comes next.

In the beginning, I leaned heavily on my best friend Brian.
I had only ever lived alone for a short time, and even in Florida
I'd had a roommate. It was an adjustment for me to be completely alone. He took my leaning on him well, having known
me for a long time and having nursed me through my back injury, coached me through my divorce, my mom's death, and saying goodbye to the center.

He was a big brother to me, inviting me to take yoga
classes, encouraging me to work out and get back into my body.
Having been a former boot camp army commander, he pushed,
prodded, kicked and cajoled me into setting up my business, my
website, and getting clear on who I was and what I wanted to
offer. Hiking up a local mountain, he'd come back after reach-
ing the top to push me towards the summit. He taught me to get
angry, to be willing to fight for what I wanted–not only on the
mountain–but in my life.

Developing my own routine, I faithfully worked out every
day, went to yoga classes and climbed that mountain. My body
changed, my energy changed. My eyes became brighter, my appearance more youthful and radiant. Six months later when my
father saw me he couldn't believe his eyes. He said he never

thought he'd see me look this way again—the way I had in my youth.

Brian was in danger of becoming the new center of my existence. I was making it on my own, but I had some serious training wheels. I would find myself depending heavily on him for emotional support. I would see my old pattern of feeling empty and using his friendship to fill that emptiness. But I wasn't ready to let go. For now, I needed him. Even if it meant I was leaning a little more than was healthy.

I started learning to appreciate the body I have. Rather than wishing my body were different, I began to appreciate it for what it was. I set out to make the most of it, rather than hide it. That meant I had to begin by accepting it the way it was. I figured out I didn't have to be model thin to look nice or have a personal sense of style. I stopped trying to look like everyone else, and started dressing in a way that made *me* feel elegant, beautiful and sexy. The way I walked, the way I held myself changed. I was starting to believe in myself.

Around this time, I ran into an old friend. We'd met during my last stay in Phoenix, recovering from my back injury. We started seeing each other, soon becoming what is commonly known as "friends with benefits." Michael and I would get together once every couple of weeks. We'd have a great time talking, laughing, and making love. When we first met, I was self-conscious about my body. He was ten years younger, and surely used to a level of perfection I couldn't match. He told me I was beautiful. That he loved my body, its shape and that it turned him on. I didn't believe him. I thought he was feeding me a line, and in my own mind I dismissed his words.

But as I, myself, began to appreciate my own body and its own unique beauty, I began to see myself from another perspective. I began to value myself just as I was. Not just in word, but in deed. All those negative thoughts that constantly plagued me just fell away. I felt a sense of peace with exactly how I looked. After so many years of looking at my body through negative eyes it was a relief to finally find this kind of peace. I was settling into myself, not only with my work and expression in the world, but with my inner world as well. A few months later, our bodies satiated and entwined, I looked up and smiled into Michael's eyes. He smiled into mine and said, "You're sexy." This time I believed him.

While my friendship with Brian was serving me in many ways, I was beginning to see it was time for the training wheels to come off. Though I had spent a lot of time on my own and had a couple of other friends, I was still reliant on him as my security blanket. If I truly wanted to be empowered, I needed to make a break from this way of relating with my best friend.

Finally, Brian and I simply stopped hanging out together for a time. Though organic and necessary, it was very painful for me, and I'm sure for Brian as well, since we'd become so close over the years.

After a week or two of being on my own I began to notice something. Being alone, the sky had not fallen. It was then that I had one of the most simple yet the most profound revelations of my life.

All this time I had been afraid to be alone. I thought if I were alone something bad would happen. The sky would fall. I would somehow be annihilated. Yet here I was on my own, estranged from my best friend. And I was okay! I hadn't collapsed into a puddle of jelly; the world had not come to an end. And though some sadness would come up from time to time, I'd come to be okay just being with myself. I enjoyed the pleasure of my own company. I had somehow learned to take care of my own needs and feel self-fulfilled.

I realized then I didn't have to have a relationship to make me happy. I could have one if I wanted one, but I didn't *need* it. And I could have any kind I wanted. I could have a teacher-student relationship, I could have an open, hippie relationship, I could have a buddy-buddy relationship. The choice was completely up to me. There was no sense of desperation. No sense that I needed to take the first thing that came along to fill the emptiness.

In truth, I wasn't empty at all. And because I wasn't empty, I didn't *need* anything to fill me. I was free to choose exactly what I wanted, if anything. In fact, I was free to have my life any way I wanted it.

With that *knowing*, came clarity. Without the desperation to fill that emptiness, my perception was no longer skewed. Instead of trying to ignore the warning signs in favor of my fairytale hopes of the future, I could see with complete objectivity. I could see the advantages and potential pitfalls of any relationship that came across my path. I had no need to move towards or away from any of them. I could just see them as they were, as clearly as if I was seeing a road map. This was the road; this was how it would go. If I wanted to take that road, I knew where it would end up. Now the choice was mine which road I wanted to take. Neither road was good or bad. Both would have high points as well as low points. It was just a question of which way I wanted to go.

It was as if choosing between chocolate or vanilla ice cream. Both were good. Both were different from each other. Neither one was wrong. But each would give a different taste. And it was clear neither one would save me. I had already saved myself. Now it was just a question of whom I wanted along for company.

What if we were treading water facing out into the vast ocean? It might appear there was nothing but emptiness for miles and miles. It might seem there was nothing and no one to save us. The world, hinting at darkness and emptiness, might give the impression that, without being saved, we would die.

If we were to see a boat coming, we might wave frantically—desperate for the person on that boat to pull us out of our watery fate and take us safely to shore. And if they were to save us, we would always go on thinking the only way to get to shore, to feel okay, is to be rescued by someone else.

But what if one day we were to realize, after searching for rescue for the umpteenth time, the shore was behind us all the time? Then we could turn around and make our *own* way to shore. We would have saved ourselves. Then, if we happened to meet someone, we wouldn't see them as the person we depended on to save our life; we would simply see them as an equal with strengths and weaknesses not dissimilar from our own.

There would be no desperation for them to behave in a certain way to make us feel okay because we'd already be there. That is what I felt I had done. I'd spent my life trying to be saved until I finally figured out I could save myself. I could turn around and make my way, stroke by stroke, to the shore.

The journey might be longer and a little harder, but it would be worth it. Because I would be on solid ground, and I would have made it all by myself. Once I got there, the choices would be all mine. I could have anything, but not be desperate for it. I would be resting on my own foundation.

Several months later, I went to Holland for my yearly visit with Steve and my other close friends. One night, Steve and I stayed up discussing the kind of person I wanted to have a relationship with. I told him I had been thinking about it.

I said, "I was thinking European, but English speaking so I wouldn't have to learn a new language." I thought a nice man from the UK would do well.

"Maybe a nice professional man." I added, getting excited.

"In the computer business. Maybe he lives in San Jose, San Francisco area. Someone who has nothing to do with personal growth or yoga. Just a really amazing, down-to-earth, naturally wise person who won't be threatened by me. He'd be so successful in his own right, he would be happy for me to do well and would encourage me to be my own person. Someone who would be my best friend, like you were, but also who would physically love me. Someone who knows about business and would guide me, but also empower me to find my own way, without trying to be the boss."

The day after I returned from Holland, I was on Facebook. About a year before I had joined eHarmony for one month and met a man online. We'd exchanged a few messages, but we'd never talked on the phone. Shortly thereafter, each of us had discontinued our respective accounts, having never exchanged addresses or any contact information, and we lost touch. I never gave it another thought.

As I opened my Facebook page this fateful day, I noticed pictures of people listed under "friends you might know." There was the man who I'd met the year before on eHarmony! I couldn't believe it! How had he ended up appearing as someone I might know? That was bizarre.

Surprised and tickled by the coincidence, I immediately sent him a message to comment on the coincidence and say hello. He replied and we began emailing. Within a week or so, we agreed to a phone call.

Imagine my shock when I picked up the phone and heard his UK accent! His name was William. I vaguely remembered he'd been from California, but didn't realize he lived just outside of San Francisco. William was in the high-tech industry and successful in his own right. Most importantly, I felt an instant rapport, as if I had always known him. We were very different, he more logical and rational, but with a deeply sensitive and insightful side. I was more sensitive and emotional, but I could relate to, and appreciate, his no-nonsense practicality. The first time we talked on the phone I cried. I told him all about me, and I didn't hold anything back. In a sense I was testing him out, to see if he could handle me. To my surprise, nothing fazed him. He wasn't uncomfortable with my emotions, my background, or my new-agey take on life. He understood it all, and could speak my language while remaining grounded in himself.

As I looked from my new perspective, I could see this was someone who could be a good complement for me. Someone who might anchor me, holding the string on a balloon, so the balloon could fly as high as she needed, without losing herself in her own flight. Here was someone who didn't need me to fulfill him, but who enjoyed my company, my take on life, and what I could add to his already complete existence.

I realized he could not and would not be the one to save me. That was up to me and me alone--always. But we could add to each other as whole individuals, rather than looking to the other to complete missing internal puzzle pieces. Here was someone who would also support me in being myself, as well as give me a swift kick in the pants when I needed one.

My relationship with William continued to develop, but very slowly. We decided to be friends and see how things would grow from there. I felt a very strong knowing that William was in my life for a reason. What the reason was I did not know, and as best as I could, I resisted the temptation to try to figure it out, with mixed results, of course. Regardless, I had met a magnificent human being who enriched my life. If I could let go of my picture of what it *had* to become, I could enjoy it for what it *was*.

In the end, I realized I don't have to make any choice. The direction that is right for me to take, will present itself with time. There is no hurry to make anything happen (though my mind still tries to convince me otherwise from time to time). I am already happy and fulfilled in the here and now. I don't need the "fairytale ending" because I already feel it right now, in the moments of my life.

And so my friends, that is how I found myself. These were my lessons on the journey to wholeness. No need for frills, or bells and whistles, or even a partner. And I can tell you from the center of my being, there is no greater feeling on Earth. The more I step into myself, the more I'm fulfilled with just me. And when I am in that place I don't need to be anywhere else.

CPSIA information can be obtained
at www.ICGtesting.com
Printed in the USA
LVHW100941090522
718247LV00003B/15

9 780983 051701